MSA
Coach

Mathematics
Grade 7

Jerome D. Kaplan, Ed.D.
Professor Emeritus,
Seton Hall University

Maryland MSA Mathematics Coach, Grade 7
11MD
ISBN# 1-58620-568-4

Editor: Adriana Velez
Cover Design: Janet Yuen
Cover Photo: CORBIS/Go Game

Triumph Learning 333 East 38th Street, New York, NY 10016-2777
© 2004 Triumph Learning, LLC
A Haights Cross Communications company

Printed in the United States of America.

10 9 8 7 6 5 4 3 2 1

Table of Contents

Standards of Learning

To the Student

This book is called a *Coach*. It will help you prepare for the Maryland Grade 7 MSA Math Test.

Here is how the *Coach* can help you:

- It shows you what math questions on the MSA Test are like.
- It tells you what you need to know to do well on the test.
- Finally, it gives you practice on the kind of math that will be on the test.

The MSA Test in Math has many **Selected-Response (SR)** questions. They are like the ones you will work with in this book. After each question there are four possible answers. Only one is correct. The others are wrong. You must mark the one correct answer after each question.

The MSA Test also has **Constructed-Response (CR)** questions. On these questions, you will have to write the answer (Part A) and then write a short explanation of why your answer is correct (Part B).

Here are some tips that will help when you work in this book and take the test:

- Read each question carefully.
- Work as carefully as you can.
- Make sure you answer the question that is asked.
- Ask yourself if the answer makes sense.
- Answer as many questions as you can.
- On selected-response questions, if you cannot decide on the answer, make the best guess you can. There is no penalty for guessing.
- On constructed-response questions, make sure you write a clear explanation for Part B.

Use these tips throughout the book and when you take the test.

You need to be able to read and write numbers into the millions.

Algebra, Patterns, and Functions

In this unit you will learn about algebra and functions. Graphing on a coordinate plane is an important topic in the study of algebra.

You will need:

- a partner
- grid paper
- a ruler
- colored pencils

Follow these steps:

1. You and your partner should each make a grid like the one at the right and plot the point P(5,4).

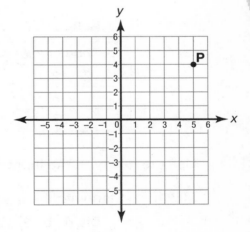

2. Working independently of your partner, draw as many rectangles as you can that measure 2 units by 3 units. Point P must be a vertex of each rectangle you draw. Label the other vertices of each rectangle with their coordinates. Use colored pencils to help tell the rectangles apart.

3. Compare your results with your partner's results. Did you find all possible rectangles? Are all the vertices labeled with the correct coordinates?

4. Compare your results with another pair of partners. How many rectangles are there in all?

Think about it:

What strategy did you use to find all the rectangles?

Compare the coordinates of the vertices in each rectangle. Which vertices have the same x-coordinates? Which have the same y-coordinates?

Standard 1.A.1.a

Lesson 1

Completing Two-Operation Function Tables

In a function table, there is a column of input numbers and a column of output numbers. A function has a rule that may involve one or more operations. Apply the rule to each input number to get an output number.

The letters x and y usually stand for input and output numbers.

Example 1

Find the output numbers in this function table.

Function Table
Rule: Divide by 3 and then add 15.

x = input numbers	y = output numbers
12	
18	
27	

STRATEGY: Use the rule with the input numbers to find the output numbers.

STEP 1: Start with the first input number.

Divide by 3: $12 \div 3 = \mathbf{4}$
Add 15 to the result: $\mathbf{4} + 15 = 19$
The first output number is 19.

STEP 2: Do the same with the other input numbers, 18 and 24.

The second input number:
Divide by 3: $18 \div 3 = \mathbf{6}$
Add 15: $\mathbf{6} + 15 = 21$

The third input number:
Divide by 3: $27 \div 3 = \mathbf{9}$
Add 15: $\mathbf{9} + 15 = 24$

SOLUTION: The output values are 19, 21, and 24.

Example 2

Find the missing values in this function table.

Rule:
Multiply by 4 and then subtract 3.

x	y
25	
30	
	177

STRATEGY: **Use the rule to find the missing output numbers. Work backward to find the missing input number.**

STEP 1: Use the rule to find the first two output numbers.

The first input number:
Multiply by 4: $25 \times 4 = 100$
Subtract 3 from the result: $100 - 3 = 97$

The second output number:
Multiply by 4: $30 \times 4 = 120$
Subtract 3 from the result: $120 - 3 = 117$

STEP 2: Work backward to find the input value for 177.

You *multiply* an input value by 4 and then *subtract* 3 to find an output value.
So, *add* 3 to an output value and then *divide* by 4 to find an input value.

Add 3: $177 + 3 = 180$
Divide the result by 4: $180 \div 4 = 45$

Use the function rule to check:
$45 \times 4 = 180$
$180 - 3 = 177$ The result checks.

SOLUTION: **The output numbers are 97 and 117, and the input number is 45.**

Sample Test Questions

1   What are the outputs in this function table?

Rule:
Multiply by 12 and then add 18.

x	y
7	
9	
11	

A   25, 27, 29

B   84, 108, 132

C   102, 124, 148

D   102, 126, 150

2   What are the output values in this table?

Rule:
Divide by 20 and then add 8.

x	y
120	
140	
160	

A   6, 7, 8

B   14, 15, 16

C   60, 70, 80

D   108, 128, 148

3   What are the input values in this table?

Rule:
Multiply by 5 and then add 3.

x	y
	13
	28
	33

A   2, 5, 6

B   2, 5, 7

C   68, 143, 168

D   24, 69, 84

4   What are the missing values in this function table?

Rule:
Divide by 8 and subtract 2.

x	y
24	
	5
96	

A   *x*: 56; *y*: 1 and 10

B   *x*: 56; *y*: 1 and 12

C   *x*: 40; *y*: 3 and 12

D   *x*: 40; *y*: 1 and 10

5 Louis completed this function table. He forgot to label the rule, which has two operations.

x	y
15	32
20	42
25	52

Look for patterns in the table. What is the output number if the input number is 45?

Brief Constructed Response

A function has this rule: Multiply by 7 and add 6.

Part A Use the rule to complete this function table.

x	y
24	
50	
	391

Part B • Use what you know about function tables to explain why your input and output answers are correct. Use words and/or numbers to support your explanation.

Lesson 2

Evaluating Expressions

You can use key words in a word expression to help you translate it into an algebraic expression with symbols. You can use algebraic expressions to represent unknown quantities.

Example 1

Write an algebraic expression for this:

the product of a number and seven tenths, increased by 9

STRATEGY: **Translate each of the key words into symbols.**

STEP 1: The *number* is the unknown. Choose a letter—or **variable**—to represent this unknown number.

Let *n* represent the number.

STEP 2: Use the key words to choose the operations.

The word *product* indicates multiplication.
So write the product of a number and seven tenths as $n \times 0.7$ or $0.7n$.

The words *increased by* indicate addition.
So write $0.7n$ increased by 9 as $0.7n + 9$.

SOLUTION: **"The product of a number and seven tenths, increased by 9" becomes $0.7n + 9$.**

Example 2

Write an algebraic expression for this:

four less than half a number

STRATEGY: **Translate each of the key words into symbols.**

    STEP 1: The number is the unknown. Choose a variable.

        Let x represent the number.

    STEP 2: Use the key words to choose the operations.

        The words *half a number* indicate multiplication of the number by $\frac{1}{2}$.

        So write half a number as $\frac{1}{2}x$.

        The words *four less than* indicate subtraction of 4.

        So write four less than $\frac{1}{2}x$ as $\frac{1}{2}x - 4$.

SOLUTION: **"Four less than half a number" becomes $\frac{1}{2}x - 4$.**

To evaluate an expression, replace the variable with a specific number and do the math.

Example 3

Evaluate $12a - 2$ when $a = \frac{3}{4}$.

STRATEGY: **Substitute and compute.**

    STEP 1: Substitute $\frac{3}{4}$ for a.

        $12a - 2 = 12(\frac{3}{4}) - 2$

    STEP 2: Compute the answer.

        $12(\frac{3}{4}) - 2 = 12 \times \frac{3}{4} - 2 = 9 - 2 = 7$

SOLUTION: **The result is 7.**

Example 4

A phone company uses this expression to calculate the cost of a phone call.

$$1.50 + 0.10m$$

$1.50 is a fixed cost, and m is the number of minutes of the call. Use the expression to find the cost of a phone call that lasts 35 minutes.

STRATEGY: **Substitute and compute.**

STEP 1: Substitute.
$$1.50 + 0.10m = 1.50 + 0.10(35)$$

STEP 2: Compute the answer.
$$1.50 + 0.10(35) = 1.50 + 3.50 = 5.00$$

SOLUTION: **The cost is $5.**

Sample Test Questions

Represent each word expression in Questions 1–4 with an algebraic expression.

1 Which expression shows a number decreased by 0.125?

  A $0.125 - x$

  B $x - 0.125$

  C $x \div 0.125$

  D $0.125 \div x$

2 Which expression shows the sum of a number and 11?

  A $11a$

  B $11 - a$

  C $a - 11$

  D $a + 11$

3 Which expression shows 18 increased by the quotient of a number and 7?

  A $18 - n \times 7$

  B $18 + n \times 7$

  C $18 + n \div 7$

  D $n \div 7 - 18$

4 Which expression shows 15 more than the product of a number and $\frac{1}{25}$?

  A $\frac{1}{25}x + 15$

  B $\frac{1}{25} + x + 15$

  C $15 - \frac{1}{25}x$

  D $\frac{1}{25}x - 15$

Evaluate the following algebraic expressions.

5 What is the value of the expression $24x - 5$ when $x = 4$?

  A 23

  B 33

  C 91

  D 101

6 The cost of a meal at Morales' Deli depends on the weight of the main course. The expression that is used to determine the cost of a meal is

$$5 + \frac{1}{2}w$$

where $5 is a fixed cost and w is the weight of the main course in ounces. What is the cost of a meal if the main course weighs 18 ounces?

A $7

B $8

C $9

D $14

7 A taxi company uses this expression to calculate the cost of a ride:

$$0.5t + 3$$

In this expression, t is the time in minutes, and $3 is a fixed charge. What is the cost of a ride that lasts 50 minutes?

A $22

B $25

C $28

D $30

8 What is the value of the expression $18n - 13$ when $n = 11$?

17

Extended Constructed Response

Maria repairs computers. She charges $25 for a house call plus $24 per hour.

Part A   Suppose a job takes h hours. Write an expression for the amount of money Maria makes.

Part B
- Use what you know about writing mathematical expressions to explain why your answer is correct. Use words and/or numbers to support your explanation.
- How many hours would Maria have to work to make at least $100 on a repair job? Use what you know about evaluating expressions to explain why your answer is correct. Use words and/or numbers to support your explanation.

Lesson 3

Order of Operations

For an expression with several operations, in what order do you add, subtract, multiply, and divide?

The answer comes from the following four rules known as the Order of Operations. These rules are applied in the order that you see them. This means you apply Rule 1 first, then Rule 2, and so on.

Rules for Order of Operations

Rule 1: Do what is inside the parentheses first.

Rule 2: Multiply and divide before you add and subtract.

Rule 3: Multiply and divide in order from left to right.

Rule 4: Add and subtract in order from left to right.

Example 1

Solve using the order of operations.

$(4 + 8) \div 2 = ?$

STRATEGY: Apply Rules 1 to 4 in order.

STEP 1: Apply Rule 1: Do what is inside the parentheses first.

$4 + 8 = 12$

STEP 2: Complete the computation.

$12 \div 2 = 6$

SOLUTION: The answer is 6.

Example 2

$26 \div 2 \times 3 = ?$

STRATEGY: **Apply Rules 1 to 4 in order.**

   STEP 1:   Check to see what rule applies first.

   Rules 1 and 2 do not apply, but Rule 3 does: Multiply and divide in order from left to right.

   STEP 2:   Since division is on the left, divide first.

   $26 \div 2 = 13$

   STEP 3:   Multiply the result by 3.

   $13 \times 3 = 39$

SOLUTION: **The answer is 39.**

Example 3

$0.3 + 0.6 \times 7 = ?$

STRATEGY: **Apply Rules 1 to 4 in order.**

   STEP 1:   Use Rule 2: multiply and divide before you add and subtract.

   $0.6 \times 7 = 4.2$

   STEP 2:   Rule 2 says add after you multiply.

   $0.3 + 4.2 = 4.5$

SOLUTION: **The answer is 4.5.**

Example 4

$\frac{7}{10} - \frac{3}{10} + \frac{1}{10} = ?$

STRATEGY: **Apply Rules 1 to 4 in order.**

      STEP 1:   Use Rule 4: add and subtract in order from left to right.

                    For this problem, Rule 4 says to subtract first:

$$\frac{7}{10} - \frac{3}{10} = \frac{4}{10}$$

      STEP 2:   Complete the computation by adding.

$$\frac{4}{10} + \frac{1}{10} = \frac{5}{10} = \frac{1}{2}$$

SOLUTION: **The answer is $\frac{1}{2}$.**

Example 5

$14 + 2 \times 6 - 7 = ?$

STRATEGY: **Apply Rules 1 to 4 in order.**

      STEP 1:   Use Rule 2: multiply and divide before you add and subtract.

                    Multiply first: $2 \times 6 = 12$

      STEP 2:   Rewrite the problem.

$$14 + 12 - 7 = ?$$

      STEP 3:   Use Rule 4: add and subtract in order from left to right.

$$14 + 12 - 7 = 26 - 7 = 19$$

SOLUTION: **The answer is 19.**

Sample Test Questions

Use the Order of Operations Rules to find the answers.

1 $72 \div 9 - 5 + 7 = ?$

   A   9

   B   10

   C   20

   D   25

2 $0.3 \times 1.5 \div 5 = ?$

   A   0.09

   B   0.9

   C   9

   D   90

3 $4 + 8 \div (4 \div 2) = ?$

   A   6

   B   8

   C   10

   D   12

4 $7 \times 7 \div 7 = ?$

   A   0

   B   7

   C   40

   D   49

5 $\frac{13}{20} - \frac{7}{20} + \frac{3}{20} = ?$

   A $\frac{3}{20}$

   B $\frac{6}{20}$

   C $\frac{9}{20}$

   D $\frac{23}{20}$

6 $7 \times 6 \div 3 + 4 - 2 = ?$

   A   4

   B   9

   C   12

   D   16

7 $5 \times (10 + 20) = ?$

   A   35

   B   70

   C   105

   D   150

8 $5 (10 + 7) = ?$

   A   35

   B   57

   C   85

   D   95

9 $24 \div 4 \times 2 = ?$

A   2

B   3

C   8

D   12

10 $200 \div 5 \times (2 + 3) - 5 = ?$

A   0

B   95

C   105

D   195

11 $5 \times (4 - 2) \times 6 \div 3 = ?$

A   10

B   20

C   30

D   40

12 $14 \div 2 \times 2 = ?$

A   3.5

B   7

C   14

D   28

13 $0.275 + 0.125 \times 3 - 0.3 = ?$

A   0.1

B   0.35

C   9

D   11.7

14 $(8 - 3) \times 2 \div 5 - 2 = ?$

A   0

B   1

C   2

D   3

15 $100 \div 2 + 3 \times 20 = ?$

A   100

B   110

C   120

D   200

16 $15 + 3(15 - 9) \div 2 = ?$

A   24

B   34

C   54

D   108

17   What is the value of this expression?

$$20 \times 4 - 4 \div 2 + 75$$

Brief Constructed Response

Carlo wrote this expression to challenge his classmates.

$15 - 5(6 \div 2) + 7 \times 7$

Part A   Find the answer for Carlo's expression.

Part B   Use what you know about the order of operations to explain why your answer is correct. Use words and/or numbers to support your explanation.

Lesson 4

Equations and Inequalities

Variables are used in expressions and sentences to represent unknown quantities.

A sentence using = is called an equation.

Example 1

Dale wants to buy a sweater that costs $20. He has already saved $12. He can save $4 per week. Write an equation to find the number of weeks he needs to save.

STRATEGY: **Use a variable and translate the words into an equation.**

STEP 1: Use w to stand for the number of weeks Dale needs to save.

STEP 2: Write an expression for the amount he can save in w weeks.

If he saves $4 in one week, he can save $4 \times w$, or $4w$ dollars, in w weeks.

STEP 3: Write the equation.

amount of money already saved	+	amount of money saved in w weeks	=	20
12	+	$4w$	=	20

SOLUTION: **An equation that can be used to find the number of weeks Dale needs to save is $12 + 4w = 20$.**

A sentence using $<$ or $>$ is called an inequality.

Example 2

Rita rode her bicycle $9\frac{1}{4}$ miles this morning. She wants her total biking distance for the day to be greater than 16 miles. Write an inequality that can be used to find the number of miles she needs to bike.

STRATEGY: **Use a variable and translate the words into an inequality.**

STEP 1: Use m to stand for the number of miles Rita needs to bike.

STEP 2: Look for words in the problem that suggest which type of symbol ($<$ or $>$) to use in the inequality.

The words *greater than 16 miles* suggest that the symbol is $>$.

STEP 3: Write an inequality with the variable m.

miles already biked	$+$	number of miles she needs to bike	$>$	16
$9\frac{1}{4}$	$+$	m	$>$	16

SOLUTION: **An inequality that can be used to find the number of miles Rita needs to bike is $9\frac{1}{4} + m > 16$.**

Sample Test Questions

1 Two friends went out to dinner and ordered exactly the same items from the menu. Their combined tip was $4.80. Their total cost including tip was $36.80. Which equation can be used to find d, the amount each friend paid for dinner without the tip?

A $d + \$4.80 = \$36.80$

B $d - \$4.80 = \$36.80$

C $2d + \$4.80 = \$36.80$

D $2d - \$4.80 = \$36.80$

2 Sal has $10\frac{1}{2}$ feet of wire. He wants to make a crafts project that requires 18 feet of wire. Which equation can be used to find n, the number of feet of wire he needs to buy?

A $10\frac{1}{2} + n = 18$

B $10\frac{1}{2} \times n = 18$

C $n - 10\frac{1}{2} = 18$

D $n \div 10\frac{1}{2} = 18$

3 A cab company charges a flat fee of $5 and $1.25 for each mile. Kimberly paid less than $10 for a cab ride. Which inequality can be used to find m, the number of miles she rode?

A $5 + 1.25m = 10$

B $5 - 1.25m < 10$

C $5 + 1.25m < 10$

D $5m + 1.25 > 10$

4 Tim makes $4 per hour babysitting. He wants to earn more than $20 this weekend. Which sentence can be used to find h, the number of hours he will have to baby sit?

A $4 + h = 20$

B $4h = 20$

C $4 + h > 20$

D $4h > 20$

Brief Constructed Response

Ginny is participating in a 5-kilometer charity walk. She asks her friends to pledge money for each kilometer in the walk. Her goal is to raise a total of more than $20.

Part A   Use the variable m to represent the amount of money in pledges she gets for each kilometer. Write an inequality that can be used to find the amount of money in pledges she must get for each kilometer to reach her goal.

Part B   Use what you know about writing inequalities to explain why your answer is correct. Use words and/or numbers to support your explanation.

Lesson 5

Rational Numbers on a Number Line

A **r**ational number is any number that can be expressed as the ratio of two integers. Rational numbers include integers, fractions, terminating decimals, repeating decimals, and percents. Some examples of rational numbers are:

$$\frac{5}{8} \qquad 1.\overline{3} \qquad -13.75 \qquad 48\% \qquad -3\frac{3}{4}$$

Example

Each of the four letters on the number line below stands for one of these rational numbers.

$$58\% \qquad 0.182 \qquad -1\frac{2}{3} \qquad -0.812$$

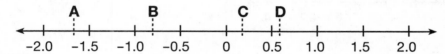

Identify the numbers represented by each letter.

STRATEGY: Change all numbers to decimals.

STEP 1: Change the percent to a decimal.
$$58\% = 0.58$$

STEP 2: Change the fraction to a decimal.
$$-1\frac{2}{3} = -1.\overline{6}$$

STEP 3: Locate the numbers.
A is between -2.0 and -1.5. The number $-1.\overline{6}$, or $-1\frac{2}{3}$, is also between -2.0 and -1.5, so A $= -1\frac{2}{3}$.
B is between -1.0 and -0.5, so B $= -0.812$.
C is between 0 and 0.5, so C $= 0.182$.
D is more than 0.5 and less than halfway between 0.5 and 1.0, so D $= 0.58$, or 58%.

SOLUTION: The four numbers represented by the letters are A $= -1\frac{2}{3}$, B $= -0.812$, C $= 0.182$, and D $= 58\%$.

Sample Test Questions

1 Which number does X represent on the number line?

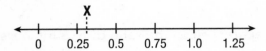

A 28%

B 3.5%

C $\frac{3}{8}$

D 0.19

2 Which number does Y represent on the number line?

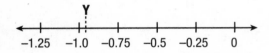

A −85%

B −850%

C $-\frac{3}{4}$

D −0.94

3 Which number does Z represent on the number line?

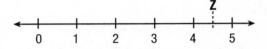

A 4.5%

B 45%

C 450%

D 4500%

4 Each of the four letters on the number line below stands for one of these numbers.

50%   −0.5 $\frac{3}{2}$ 15.5%

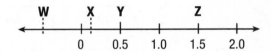

Identify the numbers represented by each letter.

A W = 50%, X = −0.5, Y = 15.5%, Z = $\frac{3}{2}$

B W = −0.5, X = $\frac{3}{2}$, Y = 50%, Z = $\frac{3}{2}$

C W = 20.5, X = 50%, Y = $\frac{3}{2}$, Z = 15.5%

D W = −0.5, X = 15.5%, Y = 50%, Z = $\frac{3}{2}$

Brief Constructed Response

Hank graphed these rational numbers on a number line.

4.25 $\qquad$ $-3\frac{3}{4}$ $\qquad$ 150% $\qquad$ $-\frac{1}{3}$

Part A This is Hank's graph.

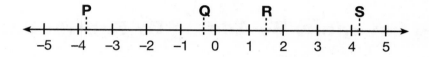

Identify the numbers represented by each letter.

Part B Use what you know about rational numbers on a number line to explain why your answer is correct. Use words and/or numbers to support your explanation.

Lesson

6

Solving Equations

"Solving" an equation means finding the number represented by the variable (usually a letter like x or y). To solve an equation, isolate the variable. This means getting the variable by itself on one side of the equation.

Solving Equations By Adding Or Subtracting

Example 1

Solve the equation $6 + N = 15$.

STRATEGY: **Isolate the variable.**

STEP 1: Start with the equation: $6 + N = 15$

STEP 2: Get rid of 6 on the lefthand side of the equation.

Subtract 6 from both sides of the equation:
$(6 - \mathbf{6}) + N = 15 - \mathbf{6}$

STEP 3: Do the math.

$(6 - 6) + N = 15 - 6$
$0 + N = 9$
$N = 9$

SOLUTION: **The solution is 9.**

Example 2

Solve the equation $z + \frac{3}{10} = \frac{4}{5}$.

STRATEGY: **Get z by itself on one side of the equation.**

Get rid of $\frac{3}{10}$ by subtracting $\frac{3}{10}$ from both sides:

$$z + \frac{3}{10} = \frac{4}{5}$$

$$z + \left(\frac{3}{10} - \frac{3}{10}\right) = \frac{4}{5} - \frac{3}{10}$$

$$z + 0 = \frac{4}{5} - \frac{3}{10}$$

$$z = \frac{4}{5} - \frac{3}{10} = \frac{8}{10} - \frac{3}{10} = \frac{5}{10} = \frac{1}{2}$$

SOLUTION: **The solution is $\frac{1}{2}$.**

Solving Equations By Multiplying

Example 3

Solve the equation $4C = 72$.

STRATEGY: **Isolate C by multiplying.**

STEP 1: Start with the equation: $4C = 72$

STEP 2: Get rid of the 4 that multiplies C.
Use the reciprocal of 4, which is $\frac{1}{4}$.
Multiply both sides by $\frac{1}{4}$. (This is the same as dividing by 4.)
$$\frac{1}{4}(4C) = \frac{1}{4}(72)$$

STEP 3: Do the math.
$$\frac{1}{4}(4C) = \frac{1}{4}(72)$$
$$\left(\frac{1}{4} \times 4\right)C = \frac{1}{4} \times \frac{72}{1}$$
$$1C = 18$$
$$C = 18$$

SOLUTION: **The solution is 18.**

Example 4

Solve: $\frac{r}{2} = 75$

STRATEGY: **Multiply both sides by 2.**

$$2(\tfrac{r}{2}) = 2(75)$$
$$r = 150$$

SOLUTION: **The solution is 150.**

Solving Equations In Two Steps: By Adding or Subtracting and By Multiplying

Example 5

Solve the equation $2t - 0.9 = 1.5$.

STRATEGY: **Isolate t. (Get t by itself on one side of the equation.)**

STEP 1: Add 0.9 to both sides:
$$2t - 0.9 + \mathbf{0.9} = 1.5 + \mathbf{0.9}$$

STEP 2: Do the math.
$$2t - 0.9 + 0.9 = 1.5 + 0.9$$
$$2t + 0 = 2.4$$
$$2t = 2.4$$

STEP 3: Multiply both sides by $\frac{1}{2}$.
$$\tfrac{1}{2}(2t) = \tfrac{1}{2}(2.4)$$

STEP 4: Do the math.
$$\tfrac{1}{2}(2t) = \tfrac{1}{2}(2.4)$$
$$t = 1.2$$

SOLUTION: **The solution is 1.2.**

Example 6

Solve: $7y + 10 = 52$.

STRATEGY: **Isolate *y*.**

    STEP 1:   Subtract 10 from both sides.

$$7y + 10 - \mathbf{10} = 52 - \mathbf{10}$$
$$7y + 0 = 42$$
$$7y = 42$$

    STEP 2:   Multiply both sides by $\frac{1}{7}$.

$$\tfrac{\mathbf{1}}{\mathbf{7}}(7y) = \tfrac{\mathbf{1}}{\mathbf{7}}(42)$$
$$y = 6$$

SOLUTION: **The solution is 6.**

Sample Test Questions

Solve for the variable in each equation.

1 $4x = 16$

A 64   C 4
B 8   D 2

2 $3x = 27$

A 3   C 9
B −3   D −9

3 $0.9 + M = 5$

A 5.9   C 4.1
B −5.9   D −4.1

4 $y + 1.3 = 2.2$

A 0.9   C 4.0
B −3.5   D −4.5

5 $2b − 7 = 11$

A −1   C 9
B −2   D −9

6 $20 + 5z = 160$

A −10   C 28
B −20   D −28

7 $-\frac{3}{20} + h = \frac{7}{10}$

A $\frac{17}{20}$ C $-\frac{1}{3}$
B $-\frac{17}{20}$ D $\frac{1}{3}$

8 $4m + 4 = 16$

A 16   C 12
B 3   D −3

9 What is the solution of this equation?

$$16 + 3y = 391$$

Brief Constructed Response

Part A   Solve the equation $7x - 6 = 85$.

Part B   Use what you know about solving equations to explain why your answer is correct. Use words and/or numbers to support your explanation.

Lesson 7

Solving Inequalities

You can solve an inequality the same way you solve an equation. The goal is the same—to isolate the variable.

Example 1

Solve: $x - 2.75 > 1.25$

STRATEGY: **Isolate the variable x.**

    STEP 1:   Write the inequality.

          $x - 2.75 > 1.25$

    STEP 2:   Get rid of the minus 2.75 by adding 2.75 to both sides.

          $x - 2.75 > 1.25$

          $x - 2.75 + \mathbf{2.75} > 1.25 + \mathbf{2.75}$

    STEP 3:   Do the math.

          $x - 2.75 + 2.75 > 1.25 + 2.75$

          $x + 0 > 4$

          $x > 4$

SOLUTION: **The solution is the set of all numbers greater than 4.**

You can show this solution on a number line.

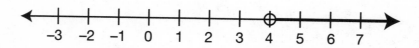

In this graph the thick line shows the solution: all numbers greater than 4. The **open dot** at 4 shows that 4 is NOT included in this solution.

Example 2

Solve: $27x \leq 162$

STRATEGY: **Isolate the variable _x_.**

 STEP 1: Write the inequality.

 $27x \leq 162$

 STEP 2: What operation do you use to isolate the variable?

 Since $27x$ shows multiplication, use the opposite operation—division. So divide by 27. (Remember: You can also look at it as multiplying by the inverse of 27, $\frac{1}{27}$.)

 STEP 3: Divide both sides of the inequality by 27 and do the computation.

 $27x \div \mathbf{27} \leq 162 \div \mathbf{27}$

 $27x$ is divided by a positive number, 27, so the $\leq$ sign does not change direction.

 $x \leq 6$

SOLUTION: **The solution is the set of all numbers less than or equal to 6.**

You can show this solution on a number line.

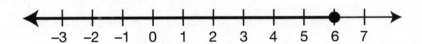

In this graph, the thick line shows the solution: all numbers less than or equal to 6. The **closed dot** at 6 shows that 6 is included in the solution.

Sample Test Questions

1 Solve for x: $3 + x > 100$

   A $x < 97$

   B $x > 97$

   C $x > 103$

   D $x < 103$

2 Solve for y: $2y \geq 32$

   A $y \leq 64$

   B $y \geq 30$

   C $y \geq 16$

   D $y \geq 12$

3 Solve for z: $3z \leq 4.2$

   A $z \leq 14$

   B $z < 1.4$

   C $z \leq 1.4$

   D $z > 1.4$

4 $10q < 150$

   A $q > 15$

   B $q < 15$

   C $q > 140$

   D $q < 140$

5 $v - 20 > 30$

   A $v > 10$

   B $v < 10$

   C $v > 50$

   D $v < 50$

6 Which graph shows the solution for this inequality?

$x + 12 \leq 14$

A

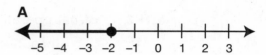

B

C

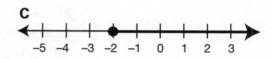

D

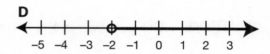

7 Which graph shows the solution for this inequality?

$4x > 12$

A

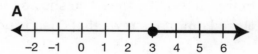

B

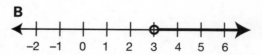

C

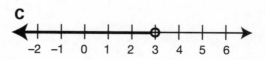

D

Brief Constructed Response

Joel decided to start a collection of baseball cards. He buys 8 baseball cards each week. He wants to have at least 40 cards in his collection. This inequality can be used to find the number of weeks it will take him to reach his goal.

$8w \geq 40$ w represents the number of weeks

Part A   Solve the inequality.

Part B   Use what you know about solving inequalities to explain why your answer is correct. Use words and/or numbers to support your explanation.

Lesson

8

Formulas

Mathematics and science are full of formulas. We need to know how to substitute into formulas to find answers to solve problems.

Example

The Nelson family drove from their home to an amusement park. Their average rate of speed was 45 miles per hour. The trip took 1.5 hours. What is the distance from the Nelson home to the amusement park?

The formula for distance is:

$$d = rt$$

d stands for the distance

r stands for the rate of speed

t stands for the amount of time the trip takes

STRATEGY: **Substitute the values from the problem in the formula.**

STEP 1: Write the formula

$$d = rt$$

STEP 2: Substitute the values into the formula.

$r = 45$ and $t = 1.5$

$d = rt = (45)(1.5)$

STEP 3: Do the math.

$d = rt = (45)(1.5) = 67.5$

SOLUTION: **The distance from the Nelson home to the amusement park is 67.5 miles.**

Sample Test Questions

1 The cost (in dollars) to rent a car at the ABC Auto Rental Company can be determined by the formula $C = 26D + 2H$, where D = number of days rented and H = number of additional hours. What is the cost of renting a car for 3 full days and 6 hours?

A $80

B $86

C $90

D $92

2 The area of a circle is given by the formula $A = \pi r^2$. The letter A stands for area, π stands for the number pi, which is approximately 3.14, and r stands for the radius of the circle. What is the area of a circle whose radius is 30 meters?

A 2826 m²

B 706.5 m²

C 353.25 m²

D 300 m²

3 A formula for finding the volume of a cone is $V = \frac{1}{3}Bh$, where B stands for the area of the cone's circular base and h stands for the cone's height. If a cone has a base with an area of 28.26 in² and a height of 6 in., find its volume.

A 28.26 cu. in.

B 34.26 cu. in.

C 56.52 cu. in.

D 169.56 cu. in.

4 The cost of recording a song at the Music Maker is $20 per song, plus $2 for each minute of tape used. The formula $C = 20 + 2m$, where C is the cost of the song and m is the number of minutes of tape used, can be used to find the cost of recording a song. If Devon's band recorded one song and used 15 minutes worth of tape, how much was the total cost?

A $30

B $40

C $45

D $50

5 A zebra can run at a speed of 40 miles per hour. If the zebra could run at that speed for $\frac{3}{5}$ of an hour, what distance would the zebra run? Use the formula $d = rt$, where d is the distance, r is the rate of speed, and t is the amount of time.

A 8 miles

B 24 miles

C 30 miles

D 40 miles

6 Kathy charges $5 per hour to baby sit plus $4 for carfare to get to and from a babysitting job. The formula she uses to determine the total amount she earns is $E = 5n + 4$, where E stands for her total earnings and n stands for the number of hours she baby sits. How much will Kathy earn if she baby sits for 4.5 hours?

A $13.50

B $22.50

C $26.50

D $36.50

7 Mrs. Harold owns a rectangular lot that is 20.5 yards long and 15 yards wide. She wants to build a fence around the lot. A formula for the perimeter is $P = 2(l + w)$ where P stands for the perimeter, l stands for the length, and w stands for the width. How many yards of fencing will she have to buy?

Brief Constructed Response

The formula for finding the volume of a cylinder is $V = Bh$, where B stands for the area of the cylinder's circular base and h stands for the cylinder's height. A storage tank has the shape of a cylinder. The area of its base is 31.4 square feet, and its height is 6.5 feet.

Part A   What is the volume of the storage tank?

Part B   Use what you know about using formulas to explain why your answer is correct. Use words and/or numbers to support your explanation.

Lesson

9

Graphs on the Coordinate Plane

What is an **ordered pair** of numbers?

An ordered pair of numbers is a set of 2 numbers such as (−4,2).

- −4 is the first number of the ordered pair.
- 2 is the second number of the ordered pair.
- The first number is called the *x*-coordinate.
- The second number is called the *y*-coordinate.

Each ordered pair can be represented by a point on a grid like the one shown below:

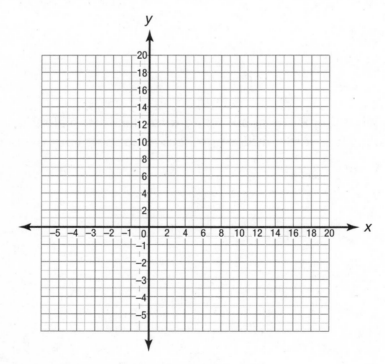

On this grid, the lines with arrows are called **axes**.

- The left-right axis is called the *x*-axis.
- The up-down axis is called the *y*-axis.
- The point where the two axes cross (marked 0) is called the **origin**.

Example

Locate the points on the grid for these ordered pairs:

A(−4,2), B(−2,0), C(0,−2), D(2,−4).

STRATEGY: **Use each number to find the exact location on the grid.**

STEP 1:   Locate point A. Start at the origin. Remember, the origin is the place where the x-axis and the y-axis meet.

STEP 2:   The x-coordinate is −4. Since the x-coordinate is negative, move 4 units to the left of the origin.

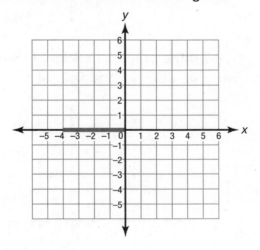

STEP 3:   The y-coordinate is 2. Since the y-coordinate is positive, move 2 units up.

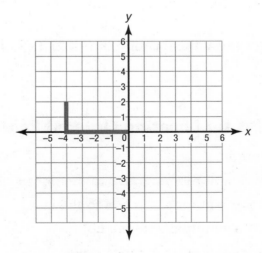

STEP 4:   Place a dot at this point. The dot shows the location of point A.

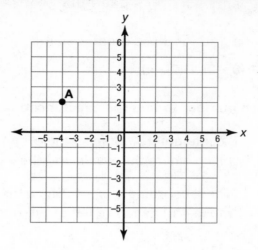

STEP 5:   Repeat the process in Steps 1 through 4 to locate points B(−2,0), C(0,−2), and D(2,−4).

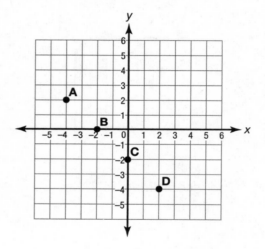

SOLUTION: The dots show the location of (−4,2), (−2,0), (0,−2), and (2,−4).

Rules for Locating Ordered Pairs on a Grid

Start at the origin.

- For positive x-numbers, move to the **right**.
- For negative x-numbers, move to the **left**.
- For positive y-numbers, move **up**.
- For negative y-numbers, move **down**.

Sample Test Questions

1 Which letter identifies the ordered pair (5,2)?

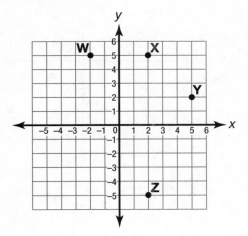

A W

B X

C Y

D Z

2 Which letter identifies the ordered pair (−4,0)?

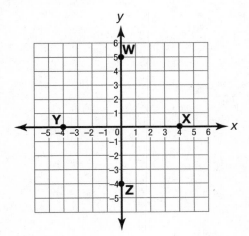

A W

B X

C Y

D Z

3 Which letter identifies the ordered pair (−3,−2)?

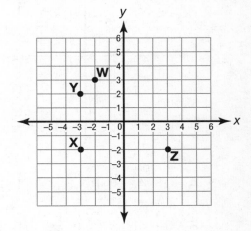

A W

B X

C Y

D Z

4 Which letter identifies the ordered pair (−1,−4)?

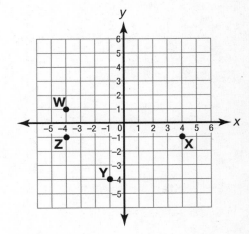

A W

B X

C Y

D Z

5 What are the coordinates of the points shown?

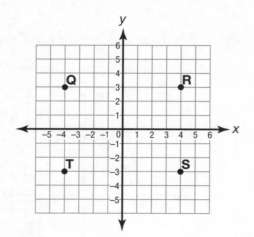

A Q(−4,−3), R(4,3), S(−3,4), T(−4,−3)

B Q(−4,3), R(4,3), S(−3,4), T(−3,−4)

C Q(−4,3), R(4,3), S(4,−3), T(−4,−3)

D Q(−4,3), R(3,4), S(4,−3) T(−3,−4)

6 What are the coordinates of the points shown?

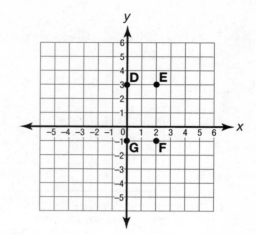

A D(3,0), E(2,3), F(2,0), G(0,−1)

B D(0,3), E(2,3), F(2,−1), G(0,−1)

C D(0,3), E(2,3), F(2,−1), G(−1,0)

D D(3,0), E(3,2), F(−1,2), G(−1,0)

Brief Constructed Response

Points J, K, L, M and N are on this coordinate grid.

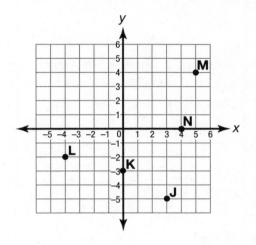

Part A   Name the coordinates of point L.

Part B   Use what you know about graphing on the coordinate plane to explain why your answer is correct. Use words and/or numbers to support your explanation.

Lesson 10

Identifying Change in a Table of Values

A function rule can be expressed as an equation in which *x* represents the input values and *y* represents the output values. The table below shows how to substitute input values in an equation to find output values. The input and output values form ordered pairs.

Input: x	Rule: y = 2x + 1	Output: y	Ordered Pair: (x,y)
0	y = 2(0) + 1 = 0 + 1 = 1	1	(0,1)
1	y = 2(1) + 1 = 2 + 1 = 3	3	(2,3)
2	y = 2(2) + 1 = 4 + 1 = 5	5	(3,5)

The ordered pairs show that as the input values increase, the output values also increase.

Example

A function has the rule $y = -3x$. Use the input values 1, 3, and 5 to find output values. How do the output values change as the input values increase?

STRATEGY: **Substitute input values in the function rule and look at the output values.**

STEP 1: Substitute input values to find output values.

Use a table to organize the substitution.

Input: x	Rule: y = –3x	Output: y	Ordered Pair: (x,y)
1	y = −3(1) = −3	−3	(1,−3)
3	y = −3(3) = −9	−9	(3,−9)
5	y = −3(5) = −15	−15	(5,−15)

STEP 2: Look at the ordered pairs to see how the output values change.

As the input values increase (1, 3, 5), the output values decrease (−3, −9, −15).

SOLUTION: **The output values decrease.**

Sample Test Questions

In Questions 1–4, use the information in the table to decide which statement is true.

1

x	y = 2x − 2	y	(x,y)
1	y = 2(1) − 2	0	(1,0)
2	y = 2(2) − 2	2	(2,2)
3	y = 2(3) − 2	4	(3,4)

A As x-values increase, y-values increase.

B As x-values increase, y-values decrease.

C As x-values increase, y-values do not change.

D As x-values decrease, y-values increase.

3

x	y = 0x + 2	y	(x,y)
3	y = 0(3) + 2	2	(3,2)
6	y = 0(6) + 2	2	(6,2)
9	y = 0(9) + 2	2	(9,2)

A As x-values increase, y-values increase.

B As x-values increase, y-values decrease.

C As x-values increase, y-values do not change.

D As x-values decrease, y-values increase.

2

x	y = −1x + 5	y	(x,y)
2	y = −1(2) + 5	3	(2,3)
4	y = −1(4) + 5	1	(4,1)
6	y = −1(6) + 5	−1	(6,−1)

A As x-values increase, y-values increase.

B As x-values increase, y-values decrease.

C As x-values increase, y-values do not change.

D As x-values decrease, y-values decrease.

4

x	y = x − 8	y	(x,y)
0	y = 0 − 8	−8	(0,−8)
3	y = 3 − 8	−5	(3,−5)
6	y = 6 − 8	−2	(6,−2)

A As x-values increase, y-values increase.

B As x-values increase, y-values decrease.

C As x-values increase, y-values do not change.

D As x-values decrease, y-values increase.

Brief Constructed Response

This table shows the input values for a function with the rule $y = 8 - x$.

x	$y = 8 - x$	y	(x,y)
2	$y = 8 - 2$		
4	$y = 8 - 4$		
5	$y = 8 - 5$		

Part A   As the x-values increase, tell whether the y-values increase, decrease, or do not change.

Part B   Use what you know about how values change in a table to explain why your answer is correct. Use words and/or numbers to support your explanation.

Progress Check for Lessons 1–10

1 What are the missing output values in this function table? The rule is $y = x \div 5 + 18$.

x = input numbers	y = output numbers
100	
150	
175	

A 20, 30, 35

B 38, 48, 58

C 38, 48, 53

D 38, 48, 68

2 Which expression shows thirteen less than the product of a number and six?

A $6x - 13$

B $13 - 6x$

C $6x + 13$

D $x + 6 - 13$

3 Chevon's weekly earnings for her paper route can be found by evaluating the expression $11.50 + 0.05p$, where $11.50 is a fixed rate she receives for completing her route, and $0.05 is the amount she earns for each paper she delivers. How much will Chevon earn if she delivers a total of 119 newspapers this week?

A $5.95

B $16.75

C $17.45

D $18.05

4 What is the value of this expression?

$$125 \div 5(1 + 4) - 3$$

A 2

B 25

C 122

D 147

5 Manny wants to buy a CD that costs $18.50, including tax. He has already saved $11. He can save $2.50 per week. Which equation can be used to find w, the number of weeks he will have to save to buy the CD?

A $18.50 = 2.50w - 11$

B $18.50 = 2.50w + 11$

C $18.50 = 11 - 2.50w$

D $18.50 = (11 + 2.50)w$

6 Jennifer wants to buy some colored pencils that cost $1.25 each. She wants her total purchase to be less than $20. Which mathematical sentence can be used to find n, the number of pencils she can buy?

A $1.25n = 20$

B $1.25n > 20$

C $1.25n < 20$

D $n \div 1.25 < 20$

7 Each of the four letters on the number line below stands for one of these numbers.

$$250\% \qquad -2\frac{1}{2} \qquad 1.9 \qquad -1.25$$

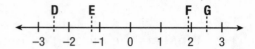

Identify the numbers represented by each letter.

A $D = 250\%$, $E = -2\frac{1}{2}$, $F = 1.9$, $G = -1.25$

B $D = 250\%$, $E = 1.25$, $F = -2\frac{1}{2}$, $G = 1.9$

C $D = -2\frac{1}{2}$, $E = 1.9$, $F = 250\%$, $G = -1.25$

D $D = -2\frac{1}{2}$, $E = -1.25$, $F = 1.9$, $G = 250\%$

8 Solve the equation: $n + \frac{2}{5} = \frac{7}{10}$

A $\frac{1}{10}$

B $\frac{3}{10}$

C $\frac{9}{15}$

D $\frac{9}{10}$

9 What is the solution of the equation $5x - 40 = 90$?

10 What is the solution of the inequality $4a < 5.6$?

A $a = 1.4$

B $a < 1.4$

C $a > 1.4$

D $a > 1.6$

11 Which graph shows the solution of this inequality?

$$m + 8 \geq 10$$

A

B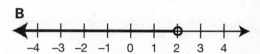

C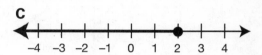

D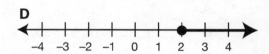

12 A train went past Jimmy's house at the rate of 66 miles per hour. How far will the train travel in $1\frac{1}{4}$ hours?

A 17 miles

B 51.5 miles

C 82.5 miles

D 96 miles

13 Which set of ordered pairs all lie on this straight line?

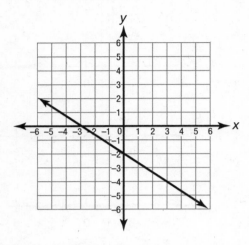

A (−3,0), (−6,2), (0,2), (3,−4)

B (−3,0), (6,2), (0,−2), (3,−4)

C (3,0), (−6,2), (0,−2), (3,4)

D (−3,0), (−6,2), (0,−2), (3,−4)

14 Use the information in the table to decide which statement is true.

x	y = 6 – x	y	(x,y)
2	y = 6 − 2	4	(2,4)
4	y = 6 − 4	2	(4,2)
6	y = 6 − 6	0	(6,0)

A As x-values increase, y-values increase.

B As x-values increase, y-values decrease.

C As x-values increase, y-values do not change.

D As x-values decrease, y-values decrease.

Constructed Response Questions

Brief Constructed Response

1 A formula for finding the total cost of an item including sales tax is $T = (1 + r)p$ where T is the total cost, r is the tax rate, and p is the price of the item before tax.

Part A A rug has a price of $140 before tax. Find the total cost if the sales tax is 0.05.

Part B Use what you know about working with formulas to explain why your answer is correct. Use words and/or numbers to support your explanation.

2 A soccer team is planning an awards banquet. The restaurant will rent its banquet hall to the team if they can guarantee that more than 100 people will attend. Each table in the banquet hall seats 6 people.

Part A Write an inequality to find t, the number of tables that will be needed if the team can meet the restaurant's requirement of more than 100 people.

Part B Use what you know about inequalities to explain why your answer is correct. Use words and/or numbers to support your explanation.

Extended Constructed Response

3   A function has the rule $y = 2x - 3$.

Part A   Use the rule to complete this function table.

Input **x**	Output **y**
2	
3	
4	

Part B
- Use what you know about function tables to explain why your answer is correct. Use words and/or numbers to support your explanation.
- Use your table to make a list of three ordered pairs. Then graph the points for the ordered pairs on this grid. Use words and/or numbers to explain how you graphed the points.

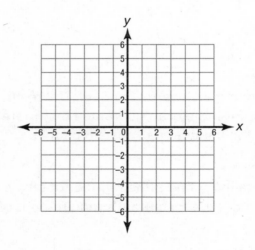

4   Dave is reading a 240-page novel. He has already read 60 pages. He reads 15 pages per hour.

Part A   Write an equation to find h, the number of hours it will take him to finish the novel.

Part B
- Use what you know about writing equations to explain why your answer is correct. Use words and/or numbers to support your explanation.
- Solve your equation to find how many hours it will take Dave to finish the novel. Then use evidence from the problem to find out how many hours in all it will take him to read the entire novel. Use words and/or numbers to support your answers.

Geometry

In this unit you will learn some concepts of geometry. When you find the reflection of a figure over the *x*- or *y*-axis, the corresponding vertices are the same distance from the axis of reflection.

You will need:

- a partner
- grid paper
- a ruler
- colored pencils

Follow these steps:

1. This grid shows the reflection of triangle *ABC* over the *y*-axis. The reflected image is triangle *A'B'C'*.

   Notice that both *A* and *A'* are 4 units from the *y*-axis, both *B* and *B'* are 5 units from the *y*-axis, and both *C* and *C'* are 2 units from the *y*-axis.

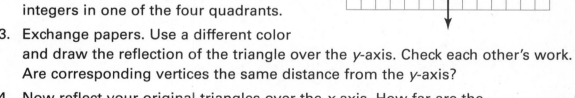

2. You and your partner each make your own coordinate grid. Draw a triangle with vertices whose coordinates are integers in one of the four quadrants.

3. Exchange papers. Use a different color and draw the reflection of the triangle over the *y*-axis. Check each other's work. Are corresponding vertices the same distance from the *y*-axis?

4. Now reflect your original triangles over the *x*-axis. How far are the corresponding vertices from the *x*-axis?

Think about it:

Sometimes a reflection is called a flip. Describe the flip in the reflections you drew.

How do the coordinates of the corresponding vertices of the triangle and its reflected image compare?

Lesson
11

Special Angles

You need to know how to recognize several special angles and their properties.

Interior and Exterior of an Angle

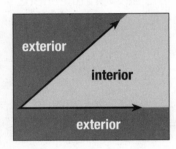

Interior of an angle: the part of the plane *between* the two sides of the angle.

Exterior of an angle: the part of the plane *outside* the two sides of the angle.

The interior of an angle, the angle itself, and the exterior of an angle make up the whole plane.

Adjacent Angles

Adjacent angles: Two angles that have a common side but no common interior parts.

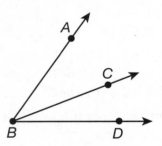

∠ABC and ∠CBD are adjacent angles. They have common side *BC* and no common interior parts.

∠ABC and ∠ABD are not adjacent angles. They have common side *BA*, but the interior of angle *ABC* is also part of the interior of angle *ABD*.

Supplementary and Complementary Angles

Supplementary angles: Two angles are supplementary if the measures of their angles add up to 180 degrees (180°).

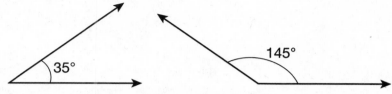

Example of two supplementary angles

If two adjacent angles form a straight line, then they are supplementary.

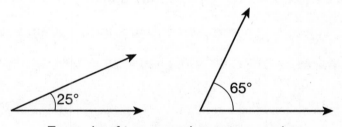

$$a + b = 180°$$

∠AZB and ∠BZC are supplementary.

Complementary angles: Two angles are complementary if the measures of their angles add up to 90 degrees (90°).

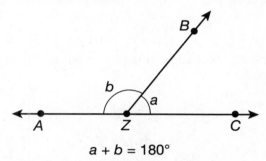

Example of two complementary angles

The acute angles of a right triangle are complementary.

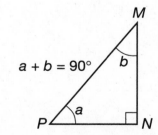

∠NPM and ∠NMP are complementary.

Vertical Angles

Vertical angles are two nonadjacent angles formed when two lines intersect.

Two pairs of vertical angles are formed when two lines intersect.

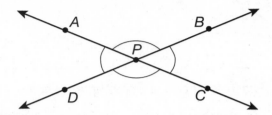

∠APB *and* ∠DPC *are vertical angles—*
so are ∠APD *and* ∠BPC.

Vertical angles are congruent. So, angle *APB* is congruent to angle *DPC*, and angle *APD* is congruent to angle *BPC*.

Example 1

If the measure of ∠*ABC* equals 20° and it is complementary to ∠*QXR*, then what is the measure of ∠*QXR*?

STRATEGY: **Use the definition of complementary angles.**

The measures of two complementary angles add up to 90°.

SOLUTION: **So, the measure of ∠*QXR* equals 90 − 20 = 70°.**

Example 2

Lines *m* and *n* intersect. Use only the angles marked with numbers to identify a pair of angles that are:

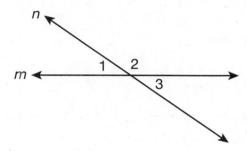

a) adjacent angles

b) vertical angles

c) supplementary angles

STRATEGY: **Use the definitions given in the lesson.**

a) Adjacent angles have a common side but no common interior parts.

SOLUTION: ∠1 and ∠2 are adjacent angles. ∠2 and ∠3 are also adjacent angles.

b) Vertical angles are two nonadjacent angles formed by two intersecting lines.

SOLUTION: ∠1 and ∠3 are vertical angles.

c) Two angles are supplementary if their measures add up to 180 degrees (180°).

Remember, if two adjacent angles form a straight line, they are supplementary.

SOLUTION: **There are two pairs of angles (marked with numbers) that form a straight line and so are supplementary: ∠1 and ∠2, and ∠2 and ∠3**

Example 3

Lines *j*, *k*, and *l* intersect as shown. Lines *j* and *k* form right angles.

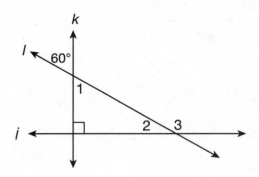

Find the measures of ∠1, ∠2, and ∠3.

STRATEGY: **Use what you know about the measures of vertical, complementary, and supplementary angles.**

STEP 1: The 60° angle and ∠1 are vertical angles.

Vertical angles are congruent. Therefore, they have the same measure.
So, the measure of ∠1 is 60°.

STEP 2: The lines form a right triangle.

∠1 and ∠2 are the acute angles of the right triangle, and the acute angles of a right triangle are complementary.
Since ∠1 has a measure of 60°, the measure of ∠2 = 90° − 60°, or 30°.

STEP 3: Adjacent angles ∠2 and ∠3 form a straight line, so they are supplementary angles.

Since ∠2 has a measure of 30°, the measure of ∠3 = 180° − 30°, or 150°.

SOLUTION: **The measure of ∠1 is 60°, the measure of ∠2 is 30°, and the measure of ∠3 is 150°.**

Sample Test Questions

1 What is the sum of the measures of two angles that are complementary?

   A 60°

   B 90°

   C 120°

   D 180°

2 If ∠PQR is supplementary to ∠XYZ and the measure of ∠XYZ equals 110°, then what is the measure of ∠PQR?

   A 50°

   B 60°

   C 70°

   D 80°

3 Look at point Q in this diagram. Where is it?

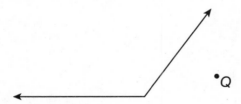

   A It is in the interior of the angle.

   B It is in the exterior of the angle.

   C It is on the angle.

   D None of the above.

Use this figure for Questions 4–7.

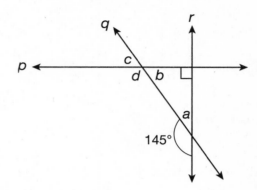

4 Which pair of angles are adjacent angles?

   A a and b

   B b and c

   C a and d

   D c and d

5 What is the measure of ∠a?

   A 35°

   B 45°

   C 90°

   D 145°

6 What is the measure of ∠b?

   A 90°

   B 55°

   C 45°

   D 35°

7 What is the measure of ∠c?

   A   35°

   B   45°

   C   55°

   D   145°

8 The measure of ∠JOT is 75°. What is the measure in degrees of an angle that is supplementary to ∠JOT?

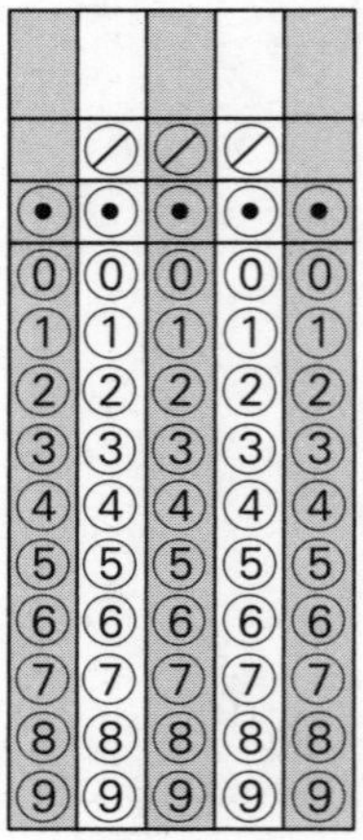

Brief Constructed Response

Willie measured an acute angle of a right triangle. Its measure was 58°.

Part A   What is the measure of the other acute angle of the right triangle?

Part B   Use what you know about the measures of special angle pairs to explain why your answer is correct. Use words and/or numbers to support your explanation.

Lesson

12

Sum of Angles of Quadrilaterals

The sum of the angles of a quadrilateral (a figure with 4 sides) is 360°.

Example 1

What is the measure of angle *T* in this diagram below?

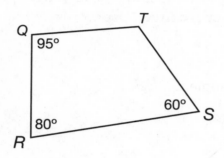

STRATEGY: **Use the fact that the sum of the angles of a quadrilateral equals 360°.**

   STEP 1:   Add the three angles you know.

   The sum of the measures of angles *Q*, *R*, and *S* is
   95 + 80 + 60 = 235

   STEP 2:   Subtract the sum from 360.

   360 − 235 = 125

SOLUTION: Angle *T* measures 125°.

Sample Test Questions

1   Find the measure of the missing angle *P* in this figure.

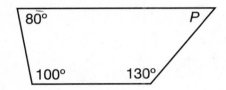

   A   60°

   B   50°

   C   40°

   D   35°

2   Find the measure of angle *Z* in the figure below.

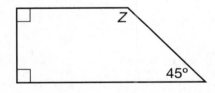

   A   135°

   B   130°

   C   125°

   D   120°

3   What is the measure of each angle of a rectangle?

   A   30°

   B   60°

   C   90°

   D   100°

4   In this figure, the measure of ∠*D* equals the measure of ∠*C*.

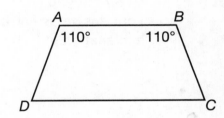

What is the measure of ∠*D*?

   A   65°

   B   70°

   C   110°

   D   140°

Brief Constructed Response

The Hickerson family bought a vacant lot in the shape of a quadrilateral to build a new home. Three of the corners of the lot were angles that measured 80°, 85°, and 100°.

Part A   What was the measure of the fourth angle of the lot?

Part B   Use what you know about the angles of a quadrilateral to explain why your answer is correct. Use words and/or numbers to support your explanation.

Lesson 13

Geometric Constructions

These are drawings and explanations of some basic constructions using a compass and ruler.

How to Construct a Circle with a Given Radius

Segment *AB* has a length of 2 centimeters.

Circle *A* has a radius of 2 centimeters.

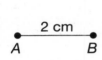 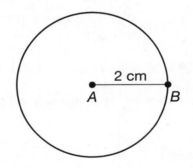

STRATEGY: **Follow these steps:**

STEP 1: Place the compass point at endpoint *A* of segment *AB*.

STEP 2: Adjust the compass so that the pencil point is at endpoint *B* of segment *AB*.

STEP 3: Using the compass point as the center, swing the compass around to make a circle.

STEP 4: Name the circle using its center point.

SOLUTION: **Segment *AB* with a length 2 centimeters has been used to construct circle *A* with radius of 2 centimeters.**

How to Construct a Segment Congruent to a Given Segment

Segment *PQ* is congruent to segment *RS*.

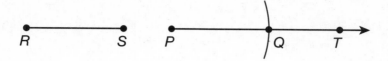

STRATEGY: Follow these steps:

STEP 1: Place the point of the compass on endpoint *R* of segment *RS*.

STEP 2: Adjust the compass so that the pencil point is at endpoint *S* of segment *RS*.

STEP 3: Using the compass setting from Steps 1 and 2, place the point of the compass on endpoint *P* of ray *PT* and draw an arc through ray *PT*.

STEP 4: Use *Q* to label the point of intersection of the ray and the arc.

SOLUTION: Segment *PQ* is congruent to segment *RS*.

How to Construct an Angle Bisector

Ray *BP* bisects ∠*ABC* into two equal angles.

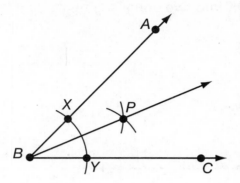

STRATEGY: **Follow these steps:**

STEP 1:   Place the compass point at the vertex *B*.

STEP 2:   Swing an arc of a circle across both sides of the angle. The arc intersects ∠*ABC* at *X* and *Y*.

STEP 3:   Place the compass point at *X* and draw an arc in the interior of the angle.

STEP 4:   Place the compass point at *Y* and draw a second arc with the same radius in the interior of the angle, intersecting the first arc at *P*.

STEP 5:   Draw ray *BP*, which is the bisector of ∠*ABC*.

SOLUTION: **The angle has been divided into two angles of equal measure. ∠*ABP* has the same measure as ∠*PBC*.**

How to Construct a Perpendicular Bisector of a Segment

Line *JK* bisects segment *MN* into two equal segments, and line *JK* is perpendicular to segment *MN*.

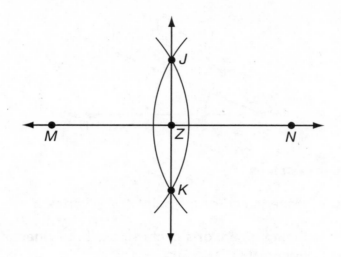

STRATEGY: **Follow these steps:**

STEP 1:   Place the compass at *N*, one of the endpoints of $\overline{MN}$.

STEP 2:   Draw an arc that intersects the segment. Make sure the compass setting is more than half the length of $\overline{MN}$.

STEP 3:   Keep the compass setting. Then place the compass at the other endpoint *M* and draw a second arc that intersects the first arc at two points. These two points are *J* and *K*.

STEP 4:   Draw the line *JK*. $\overleftrightarrow{JK}$ intersects $\overline{MN}$ at *Z* and is the bisector of $\overline{MN}$. It is also perpendicular to $\overline{MN}$.

SOLUTION: *MZ* = *ZN* and $\overleftrightarrow{JK} \perp MN$

Sample Test Questions

1 The drawing shows how to—

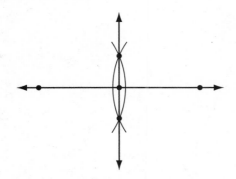

A bisect an angle.

B construct the perpendicular bisector of a segment.

C construct a line segment congruent to a given line segment.

D construct a circle with a given radius.

2 The drawing shows how to—

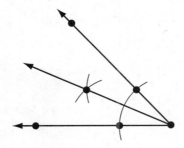

A bisect an angle.

B inscribe an angle.

C construct a perpendicular bisector.

D construct complementary angles.

3 In which construction do you divide a segment into two equal parts with a line that is perpendicular to the segment?

A bisector of an angle

B bisector of a segment

C any line that creates a 90° angle with the segment

D line parallel to a given line

4 This drawing shows how to—

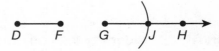

A bisect a segment.

B construct a segment congruent to a given segment.

C construct a perpendicular bisector.

D construct a circle.

5 This drawing shows how to—

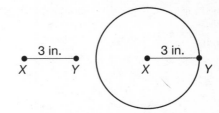

A construct a circle with a given radius.

B construct a segment congruent to a given segment.

C bisect an segment.

D bisect an angle.

Brief Constructed Response

This drawing shows a geometric construction.

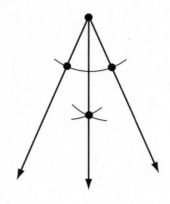

Part A   Identify the construction.

Part B   Use what you know about constructions to explain why your answer is correct. Use words and/or drawings to support your explanation.

Lesson 14

Congruent Figures

Two figures are congruent if they have the same size and shape.

If two polygons are congruent, then corresponding angles are congruent and corresponding sides are congruent.

Example 1

Triangle *ABC* is an equilateral triangle and is congruent to triangle *PQR*.

If $AB = 10$, then $QR = ?$

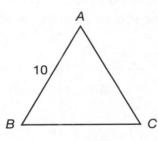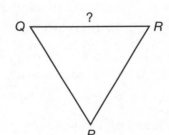

STRATEGY: Use corresponding sides of congruent figures. Notice that Triangle *PQR* is still congruent to Triangle *ABC*, even though it is flipped over.

STEP 1: What is true about the sides of an equilateral triangle?

All sides are congruent. For Triangle *ABC*:
$AB = AC = BC$

STEP 2: What is the length of the sides of Triangle *ABC*?

Since $AB = 10$, then $AC = 10$, and $BC = 10$.

STEP 3: Since the two triangles are congruent, corresponding sides are congruent:

$AB = PQ$; $AC = PR$; and $BC = QR$.

STEP 4: Combine Steps 2 and 3:

$PQ = 10$; $PR = 10$; and $QR = 10$

SOLUTION: **QR = 10**

Example 2

Pentagon *DEFGH* is congruent to pentagon *RSTVX*.

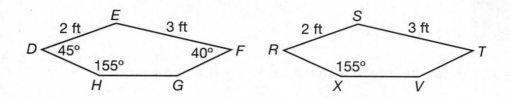

What is the measure of $\angle T$ in pentagon *RSTVX*?

STRATEGY: **Use the fact that corresponding angles in congruent figures are congruent.**

STEP 1:   Find the angle in pentagon *DEFGH* that corresponds to $\angle T$ in pentagon *RSTVX*.

Imagine placing *DEFGH* on top of *RSTVX* so that all the corresponding sides and angles match up.
$\angle F$ corresponds to $\angle T$.

STEP 2:   Use the measure of $\angle F$ to determine the measure of $\angle T$.

Since the measure of *F* is 40°, the measure of *T* is 40°.

SOLUTION: **The measure of *T* is 40°.**

Sample Test Questions

Use congruent triangles *RST* and *NOP* for Questions 1 and 2.

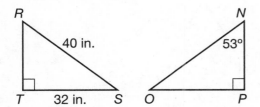

1 What is the length of side *OP* in triangle *NOP*?

    A 24 in.

    B 32 in.

    C 40 in.

    D 53 in.

2 What is the measure of angle *S* in triangle *RST*?

    A 90°

    B 53°

    C 47°

    D 37°

Use congruent quadrilaterals *JKLM* and *WXYZ* for Questions 3 and 4.

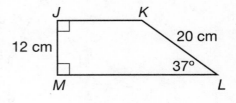

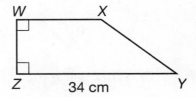

3 What is the measure of ∠*X*?

    A 37°

    B 90°

    C 133°

    D 143°

4 What is the length of side *WZ* of quadrilateral *WXYZ*?

    A 12 cm

    B 18 cm

    C 20 cm

    D 34 cm

Brief Constructed Response

Pentagon *ABCDE* is congruent to pentagon *FGHIJ*.

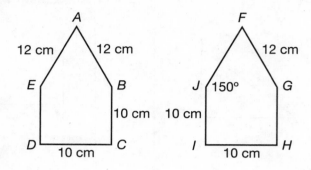

Part A   What is the measure of ∠*E*?

Part B   Use what you know about congruent figures to explain why your answer is correct. Use words and/or numbers to support your explanation.

Lesson 15

Reflections, Rotations, and Translations on a Coordinate Plane

In this lesson, all transformations will take place over the *x*-axis and the *y*-axis of a coordinate plane.

Reflections

Over the *x*-axis: If a point is the reflection of another point over the *x*-axis, then the two points lie on the same vertical line.

Over the *y*-axis: If a point is the reflection of another point over the *y*-axis, then the two points lie on the same horizontal line.

Example 1

Triangle *PQR* is reflected over the *x*-axis to form triangle *STU*. What are the coordinates of point *U*?

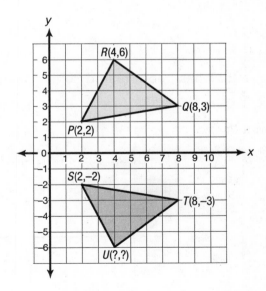

STRATEGY: Think of what happens to a point when you reflect it over the *x*-axis.

STEP 1: Check the reflections of points *P* and *Q* over the *x*-axis.

Point *P* is located at (2,2). Its reflection *S* is at (2,−2).
P is 2 units above the *x*-axis, and *S* is 2 units below the *x*-axis.
Point *Q* is located at (8,3). Its reflection *T* is at (8,−3).
Q is 3 units above the *x*-axis, and *T* is 3 units below the *x*-axis.
P and *S* are on the same vertical line.
Q and *T* are on the same vertical line.

STEP 2: Point *U* is the reflection of what point?

Since points *R* and *U* are on the same vertical line (*x* = 4), point *U* is the reflection of point *R*.

STEP 3: How many units above the *x*-axis is point *R*?

6 units

STEP 4: How many units below the *x*-axis is point *U*?

The reflection of point *U* is the same number of units below the *x*-axis as the original point is above the *x*-axis.
U is 6 units below the *x*-axis.

STEP 5: What are the coordinates of *U*?

SOLUTION: **The coordinates of *U* are: (4,−6).**

Rotations

In the diagram below, the letter T has been rotated 90° clockwise around the point of rotation.

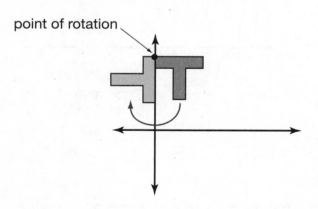

point of rotation

Example 2

Rotate △*PQR* 180° clockwise around point *Q*. What are the set of coordinates for the triangle after this rotation?

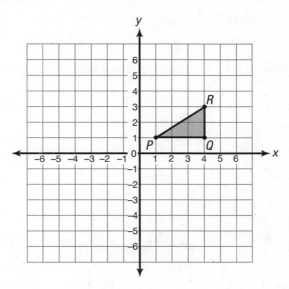

STRATEGY: Draw a new triangle with each vertex rotated 180° clockwise around point *Q*.

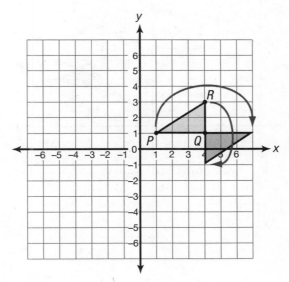

STEP 1: Start with point *Q*.

Since point *Q* is the point of rotation, it remains in the same location (4,1) after the 180° rotation.

STEP 2:   What happens to point *P* after a 180° clockwise rotation?

Point *P* is located at (1,1).
After a clockwise rotation of 180°, *P* moves to (7,1).

STEP 3:   What happens to point *R* after a 180° clockwise rotation?

Point *R* is located at (4,3).
After a clockwise rotation of 180°, *P* moves to (4,−1).

SOLUTION: **The coordinates for the triangle after the 180° rotation are (4,1), (7,1), and (4,−1).**

Translations

A translation is a slide.

Example 3

What set of coordinates will provide the vertices for the translation of △*HJK* 6 units to the left?

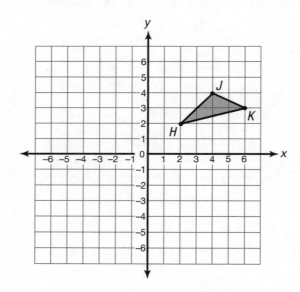

STRATEGY: **Use your pen or pencil to locate a slide of each vertex 6 units to the left.**

STEP 1:   What happens to point *H* when you slide it 6 units to the left?

Point *H* starts at (2,2). After you slide it 6 units to the left, it will end up at (−4,2).

STEP 2:   What happens to point *J* when you slide it 6 units to the left?

Point *J* starts at (4,4). After you slide it 6 units to the left, it will end up at (−2,4).

STEP 3:   What happens to point *K* when you slide it 6 units to the left?

Point *K* starts at (6,3). After you slide it 6 units to the left, it will end up at (0,3).

After the translation, the triangle looks like this:

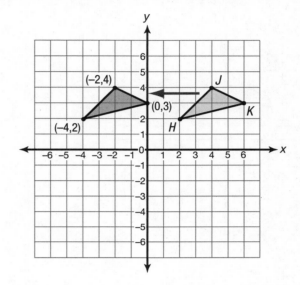

NOTE: The *x*-coordinates of the final three points are 6 less than the *x*-coordinates of the original three points. The *y*-coordinates do not change at all.

SOLUTION: **The set of coordinates is (−4,2), (−2,4), and (0,3).**

Sample Test Questions

1 △*ABC* is reflected over the *x*-axis to form △*DEF*. Point *F* is the reflection of point *C*. What are the coordinates of point *F*?

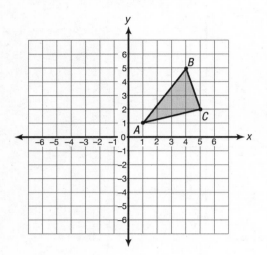

A (−2,5)

B (−5,2)

C (−5,−2)

D (5,−2)

2 If this triangle were reflected over the *y*-axis, what would be the coordinates of point *K*?

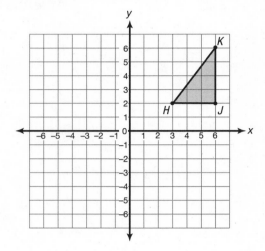

A (6,−6)

B (6,6)

C (−6,6)

D (−6,−6)

3 What set of coordinates will provide the vertices for a 90° clockwise rotation of *JKL* around point *K*?

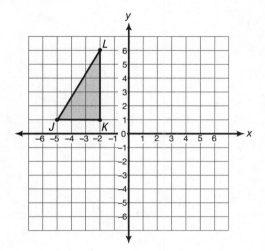

A (−2,5), (−2,1), (4,1)

B (−2,4), (−2,1), (3,1)

C (−2,5), (−2,1), (3,1)

D (−1,4), (−2,1), (3,1)

4 What set of coordinates will provide the vertices for the translation of triangle *HJK* 4 units down?

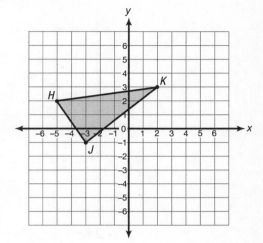

A (−5,−2), (−3,−6), (4,−1)

B (−5,2), (−3,−5), (2,−4)

C (−5,−4), (−3,5), (2,−2)

D (−5,−2), (−3,−5), (2,−1)

5 What set of coordinates will provide the vertices for a 180° clockwise rotation of triangle *RST* around point *R*?

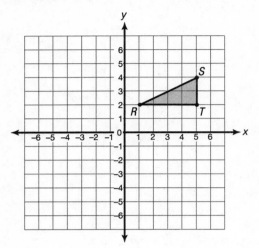

A (1,2), (−3,2), (−3,4)

B (1,2), (−3,0), (−3,2)

C (2,1), (4,5), (2,5)

D (−1,2), (−5,2), (−5,4)

6 What set of coordinates will provide the vertices for the translation of triangle *XYZ* two units to the left?

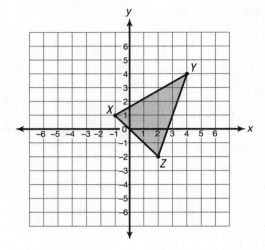

A (1,1), (6,4), (4,−2)

B (−1,3), (4,6), (2,0)

C (−3,1), (2,4), (0,−2)

D (−3,1), (1,4), (−2,0)

Brief Constructed Response

Stuart is creating a design using this triangle. He wants to reflect the triangle over the x-axis.

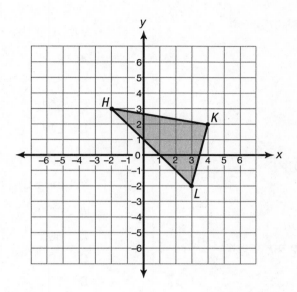

Part A   What will be the coordinates of point L after the reflection?

Part B   Use what you know about reflections over the x-axis to explain why your answer is correct. Use words and/or numbers to support your explanation.

Standard 2.0: Geometry

Progress Check for Lessons 11–15

Use this figure for Questions 1–6.

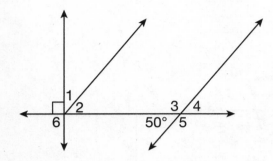

1 Which angles are adjacent?

   A ∠3 and ∠5

   B ∠1 and ∠6

   C ∠1 and ∠2

   D ∠2 and ∠3

2 Which angles are supplementary?

   A ∠1 and ∠2

   B ∠3 and ∠6

   C ∠4 and ∠5

   D ∠5 and ∠6

3 Which angles are vertical angles?

   A ∠1 and ∠2

   B ∠1 and ∠6

   C ∠3 and ∠4

   D ∠3 and ∠5

4 What is the measure of ∠4?

   A 30°

   B 40°

   C 50°

   D 60°

5 What is the measure of ∠5?

   A 40°

   B 50°

   C 120°

   D 130°

6 If the measure of ∠1 is 52°, what is the measure of ∠2?

   A 28°

   B 38°

   C 48°

   D 128°

7 What is the measure, in degrees, of ∠G in this quadrilateral?

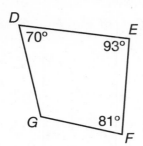

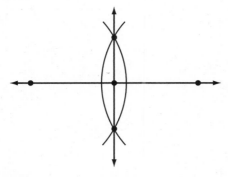

8 What construction does this drawing show?

A the bisector of an angle

B a circle with a given radius

C a segment congruent to a given segment

D the perpendicular bisector of a segment

Use this figure for Questions 9 and 10.

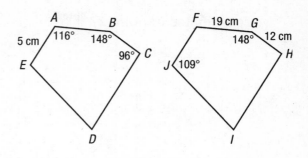

Pentagons *ABCDE* and *FGHIJ* are congruent.

9 What is the measure of ∠*H*?

A 48°

B 96°

C 109°

D 116°

10 What is the measure of side *BC*?

A 12 cm

B 15 cm

C 19 cm

D 24 cm

11 If this triangle were reflected over the *x*-axis, what would be the coordinates of point *Z*?

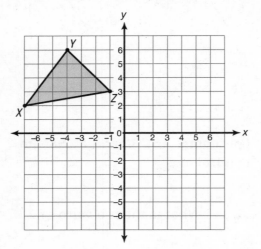

A (1,−3)   **C** (−1,3)

B (−1,−3)   **D** (1,3)

12 What set of coordinates will provide the vertices for the translation of triangle *HJK* 2 units down?

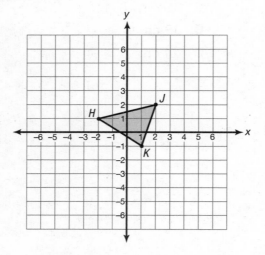

A (2,1), (−1,2), (−2,2)

B (−2,−1), (1,0), (1,−3)

C (−2,−1), (2,0), (1,−3)

D (−2,3), (2,4), (1,1)

13 What set of coordinates will provide the vertices for a 180° clockwise rotation of triangle *JKL* around point *K*?

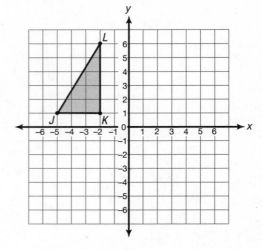

A (5,1), (2,1), (2,6)

B (−5,−1), (−2,−1), (−2,−6)

C (−2,4), (−2,1), (3,1)

D (1,1), (−2,1), (−2,−4)

Standard 2.0: Geometry

Constructed Response Questions

Brief Constructed Response

1 This map shows part of a city. Main Street and Spruce Street lie along the same straight line. Oak Street and Pine Street lie along the same straight line.

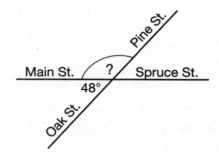

Part A What is the measure of the angle formed by Main Street and Pine Street?

Part B Use what you know about special angle pairs to explain why your answer is correct. Use words and/or numbers to support your explanation.

2   In this figure the measure of ∠P is equal to the measure of ∠O.

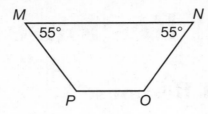

Part A   What is the measure of ∠P?

Part B   Use what you know about the measures of angles in a quadrilateral to explain why your answer is correct. Use words and/or numbers to support your explanation.

3   Copy this segment.

Part A   Construct the perpendicular bisector of the segment.

Part B   Use what you know about constructions to explain why your construction is correct. Use words and/or drawings to support your explanation.

4   These quadrilaterals are congruent.

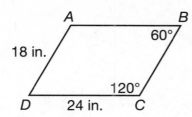
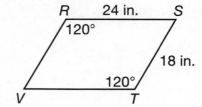

Part A   What is the measure of angle *D*?

Part B   Use what you know about angles of quadrilaterals and congruent figures to explain why your answer is correct. Use words and/or numbers to support your explanation.

Extended Constructed Response

5   Ellen graphed this triangle:

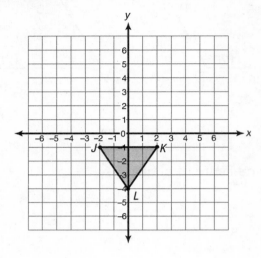

Part A   On the coordinate plane below, copy Ellen's triangle and then translate it 3 units to the left. Label the coordinates of the translated triangle.

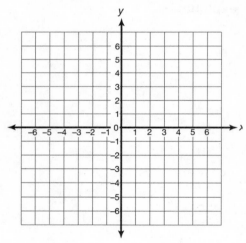

Part B
- Use what you know about translations on a coordinate plane to explain why your answer is correct. Use words and/or numbers to support your answer.
- What would be the coordinates of Ellen's triangle if you were to reflect it over the *y*-axis? Use what you know about reflections and translations on the coordinate plane to explain how a reflection is different from a translation.

Measurement

In this unit you will learn about measurement. The area of two-dimensional figures can help you understand how to find the surface area of three-dimensional figures.

You will need:

- centimeter or $\frac{1}{4}$-inch grid paper
- a partner
- a ruler
- a pencil
- scissors
- tape

Follow these steps:

1. This drawing on grid paper is called a net. If you were to cut out the figure and fold it along the dashed lines, you would form a rectangular prism, a solid figure whose six faces are rectangles. The surface area of the rectangular prism is the same as the sum of the areas of the six rectangles in the net.

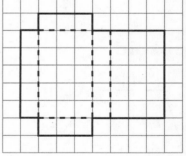

2. You and your partner each use a piece of grid paper and independently draw two copies of a net that can be folded to make a rectangular prism. Make sure to include dashed lines to indicate how the net should be folded. Make sure your net and prism are different from the one in the example above.

3. Exchange nets. Cut one of them out, fold it, and tape the edges. Is the result a rectangular prism? If so, what is the area of the net? What is the surface area of the rectangular prism?

Think about it:

If folding the net did not result in a rectangular prism, what changes do you need to make in the net?

Lesson 16

Area of Parallelograms and Trapezoids

A parallelogram is a quadrilateral with two pairs of parallel sides. A trapezoid is a quadrilateral with exactly one pair of parallel sides.

These are the formulas for the area of a parallelogram and area of a trapezoid.

Parallelogram

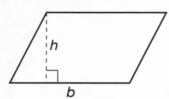

$A = bh$

(A = area, b = base, and h = height)

Trapezoid

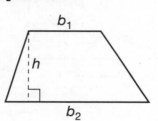

$A = \frac{1}{2}h(b_1 + b_2)$

(A = area, h = height, b_1 = one of the bases, and b_2 = the other base)

Example 1

What is the area of this parallelogram?

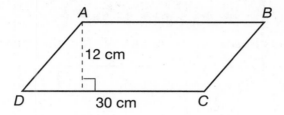

STRATEGY: Use the formula for the area of a parallelogram.

$A = bh$

base $= b = 30$ cm; height $= h = 12$ cm

$A = 30 \times 12 = 360$

SOLUTION: The area of the parallelogram is 360 square centimeters.

Remember that **area is measured in square units**, such as *square feet*, *square centimeters*, *square meters*, and so on.

There are two ways to write square. You can use either the abbreviation sq. or the exponent 2.

Square feet: write as sq. ft or ft^2

Square centimeters: write as sq. cm or cm^2

Square meters: write as sq. m or m^2

A rectangle is a special kind of parallelogram. You can think of the length as the base and the width as the height.

Example 2

A rectangular mirror measures 6 feet by 4 feet. What is the area?

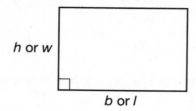

h or *w*

b or *l*

STRATEGY: **Substitute into the formula.**

Use either $A = bh$ or $A = lw$. The result will be the same.

$A = bh$ $A = lw$
    base = b = 6 ft   length = l = 6 ft
    height = h = 4 ft   width = w = 4 ft
$A = 6 \times 4 = $ **24** $A = 6 \times 4 = $ **24**

SOLUTION: **The area of the mirror is 24 ft².**

Example 3

Find the area of this trapezoid.

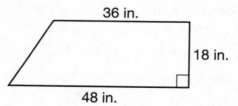

36 in.

18 in.

48 in.

STRATEGY: **Substitute into the formula.**

$A = \frac{1}{2}h(b_1 + b_2)$

In this trapezoid, one of the sides forms right angles with the bases, so the side is also the height.

height = h = 18 in., b_1 = one base = 36 in., b_2 = the other base = 48 in.

$A = \frac{1}{2} \times 18(36 + 48) = \frac{1}{2} \times 18(84) = 9(84) = 756$

SOLUTION: **The area of the trapezoid is 756 sq. in.**

Sample Test Questions

1 What is the area of a parallelogram with a height of 17 meters and a base of 24 meters?

A 41 m^2

B 204 m^2

C 408 m^2

D 816 m^2

2 What is the area of this parallelogram?

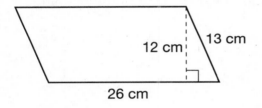

A 156 sq. cm

B 312 sq. cm

C 338 sq. cm

D 650 sq. cm

3 What is the area of a trapezoid with bases that are 7 feet and 13 feet and a height of 6 feet?

A 20 sq. ft

B 60 sq. ft

C 120 sq. ft

D 240 sq. ft

4 What is the area in square inches of this trapezoid?

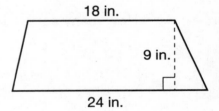

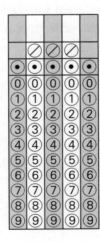

Brief Constructed Response

The side of a modern office building has the shape of a trapezoid and is completely covered with glass.

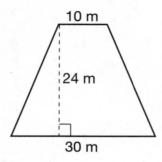

Part A   How many square meters of glass cover the side of the building?

Part B   Use what you know about finding the area of a trapezoid to explain why your answer is correct. Use words and/or numbers to support your explanation.

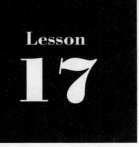

Standard 3.C.1.b

Lesson 17

Surface Area of Rectangular Prisms

The surface area of a three-dimensional figure is the area of the outside covering or surface. To find the surface area, you need to know the number of different surfaces on each figure.

Rectangular Prism

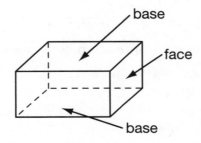

A rectangular prism has 6 faces, all rectangles. The top and bottom faces (called bases) are congruent. So are the front and back faces, as well as the two end faces.

To find the surface area of a rectangular prism, add the areas of the 6 faces.

Example

Find the surface area of this rectangular prism.

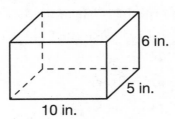

STRATEGY: Add the areas of the 6 faces, combining congruent rectangles when computing the areas.

STEP 1: Find the areas of the top and bottom faces (the two bases).

Since the two faces are congruent, they have the same length and width.

Length = 10 in. and Width = 5 in. (It does not matter which side is called the length and which is called the width.)

Area of each rectangle = Length × Width = $L \times W$ = 10 × 5 = 50 sq. in.

Area of top and bottom faces: 2 × 50 = 100 sq. in.

STEP 2: Find the area of the front and back faces.

Since the two faces are congruent, they have the same length and width.

Length = 10 in. and Width = 6 in.

Area of each rectangle = Length × Width = $L \times W$ = 10 × 6 = 60 sq. in.

Area of front and back faces: 2 × 60 = 120 sq. in.

STEP 3: Find the area of the two side faces.

Since the two faces are congruent, they have the same length and width.

Length = 5 in. and Width = 6 in.

Area of each rectangle = Length × Width = $L \times W$ = 5 × 6 = 30 sq. in.

Area of left side face and right side face: 2 × 30 = 60 sq. in.

STEP 4: Add all the areas.

100 + 120 + 60 = 280 sq. in.

SOLUTION: **The surface area of the rectangular prism is 280 sq. in.**

NOTE: A quick way to find the surface area of rectangular prisms is to use either one of these two formulas:

Surface Area = $2LW + 2LH + 2WH$

Surface Area = $PH + 2LW$

L = length of the base
W = width of the base
H = height of the prism
P = perimeter of the base

Sample Test Questions

1 Find the surface area of this rectangular prism.

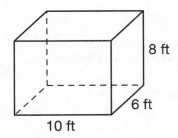

8 ft
6 ft
10 ft

A 480 sq. ft

B 376 sq. ft

C 316 sq. ft

D 256 sq. ft

2 The surface area of a rectangular prism is 5400 sq. cm. Find the height if the length of the longer side is 60 cm and the length of the shorter side is 30 cm.

A 10 cm

B 20 cm

C 30 cm

D 40 cm

3 A gift box has the shape of a rectangular prism. If the length is 8 inches, the width is 12 inches, and the height is 4 inches, how many square inches of wrapping paper will be needed to cover the box?

4 Debbie is planning to build a greenhouse in the shape of a rectangular prism. The greenhouse will be 16 feet long, 8 feet wide, and 7 feet high. The walls and roof will be made of glass. How many square feet of glass will Debbie need?

A 336 ft^2

B 464 ft^2

C 592 ft^2

D 896 ft^2

Brief Constructed Response

A manufacturer wants to produce cardboard boxes that are 15 inches long, 12 inches wide, and 6 inches high.

Part A   How many square inches of cardboard will each box have?

Part B   Use what you know about finding surface area to explain why your answer is correct. Use words, numbers, and/or drawings to support your explanation.

Lesson 18

Using Similar Polygons

Two figures are similar if they have the same shape, but different sizes.

If two figures are similar, then the following two properties are true:

1. The angles of one figure are congruent to the angles of the second figure—that is, their degree measures are the same.

2. The corresponding sides of the two figures are proportional.

This lesson applies the second property.

Example

What is the length of $\overline{RT}$ if △*DEF* is similar to △*RST*?

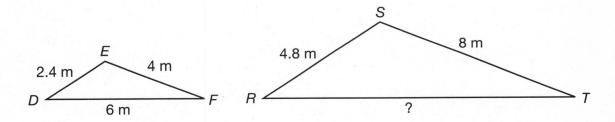

STRATEGY: **Use ratios to solve the problem.**

STEP 1: Find the sides of the two triangles that correspond to each other.

$\overline{ED}$ corresponds to $\overline{SR}$.

$\overline{EF}$ corresponds to $\overline{ST}$.

$\overline{DF}$ corresponds to $\overline{RT}$.

STEP 2: Set up ratios for the corresponding sides of $\triangle DEF$ and $\triangle RST$.

$$\frac{ED}{SR} = \frac{2.4}{4.8} = \frac{1}{2}$$

and

$$\frac{EF}{ST} = \frac{4}{8} = \frac{1}{2}$$

The ratio of the sides of $\triangle DEF$ to the corresponding sides of $\triangle RST$ is 1 to 2.

STEP 3: Set up the ratio using the unknown side $\overline{RT}$.

$$\frac{DF}{RT} = \frac{1}{2}$$

STEP 4: Substitute the length for DF.

$$\frac{6}{RT} = \frac{1}{2}$$

STEP 5: Solve for RT.

$$RT = 12$$

SOLUTION: **The length of $\overline{RT}$ is 12 meters.**

Sample Test Questions

1 △*PQR* is similar to △*XYZ*. What is the length of *YZ*?

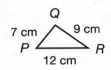

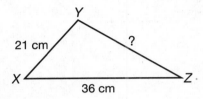

A 20 cm

B 24 cm

C 27 cm

D 30 cm

2 Figure *ABCDE* is similar to figure *VWXYZ*. What is the length of segment *YZ*?

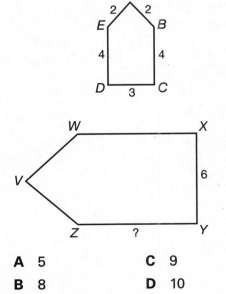

A 5   **C** 9

B 8   **D** 10

3 Triangle *ABC* is similar to triangle *XYZ*. What is the length of segment *BC*?

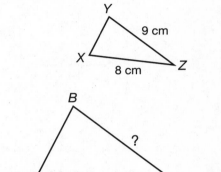

A 4.5 cm   **C** 16 cm

B 14 cm   **D** 18 cm

4 A 20-in. by 30-in. photo was proportionally reduced in size. What is the length of the unmeasured side?

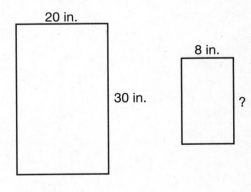

A 8 in.

B 10 in.

C 12 in.

D 18 in.

Brief Constructed Response

These octagons are similar.

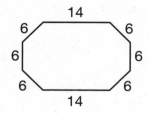 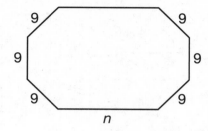

Part A   What is the length of the segment labeled *n*?

Part B   Use what you know about similar figures to explain why your answer is correct. Use words and/or numbers to support your explanation.

Lesson 19

Scale Drawings

Scale drawings and **scale models** make it possible to show objects accurately that cannot be drawn to the correct size—they are too big, or too small, or too complex. Common examples of scale drawings and models are maps, architects' drawings, and models of homes and buildings.

In all cases, there is a numerical **scale** that is used to compute the actual dimensions. A scale is a ratio—the ratio between the dimensions of the drawing and the actual dimensions of the object.

Example

On a map, Steve measured the straight-line distance between Baltimore and his home town. It is 2.5 centimeters. The scale on the map shows 1 cm = 12 kilometers. What is the actual distance from Baltimore to Steve's town?

STRATEGY: **Make a proportion and solve it.**

STEP 1: Use the scale to set up the proportion.

$$\frac{1 \text{ cm}}{12 \text{ km}} = \frac{2.5 \text{ cm}}{N \text{ km}}$$

STEP 2: Solve the proportion by cross-multiplying.

$N \times 1 = 12 \times 2.5 = 30$

$N = 30$ km

SOLUTION: **The actual distance from Baltimore to Steve's home is 30 km.**

Sample Test Questions

1 Harold made a scale drawing of his bedroom. He used the scale $\frac{1}{4}$ inch = 1 foot. The length of his bedroom in the drawing is 4 inches. What is the actual length of his bedroom?

A 1 ft

B 12 ft

C 16 ft

D 20 ft

2 The students in Greg's class made a scale drawing of the school field. The dimensions of the field in the drawing are 40 cm by 20 cm. If the scale is 1 cm = 2 m, what are the actual dimensions of the field?

A 60 m by 30 m

B 80 m by 60 m

C 80 m by 40 m

D 400 m by 200 m

3 Sonya made a model of the new town hall for her town. Her scale is $\frac{3}{4}$ in. = 1 ft. If the height of the building in the model is 48 inches, what is the actual height of the building?

A 36 ft

B 48 ft

C 64 ft

D 72 ft

4 Find the actual distance (in miles) between two cities given this information:

Distance on map: $3\frac{1}{2}$ in.

Scale: $\frac{1}{2}$ in. = 40 miles

116

Brief Constructed Response

The distance on a map between two cities is 6.5 cm. The scale of the map is
1 cm = 8 km.

Part A   What is the actual distance between the two cities?

Part B   Use what you know about scale drawings to explain why your answer is
correct. Use words and/or numbers to support your explanation.

Standard 3.0: Measurement

Progress Check for Lessons 16–19

1 What is the area of this parallelogram?

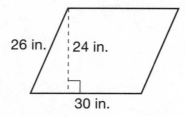

A 780 in.²

B 720 in.²

C 624 in.²

D 360 in.²

2 What is the area of this trapezoid?

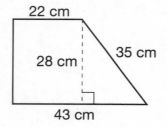

A 308 sq. cm

B 392 sq. cm

C 490 sq. cm

D 910 sq. cm

3 These hexagons are similar. What is the length of the side labeled *x*?

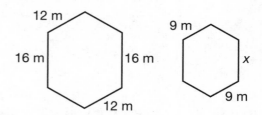

A 9 m

B 12 m

C 16 m

D 18 m

4 What is the surface area, in square inches, of this rectangular prism?

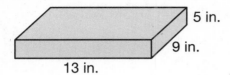

5 in.
9 in.
13 in.

5 The scale on a blueprint of a house is $\frac{1}{4}$ in. = 1 ft. On the blueprint, the front of the house is $5\frac{1}{4}$ inches wide. What is the actual width of the house?

A 20 ft

B 21 ft

C 22 ft

D 23 ft

Standard 3.0: Measurement

Constructed Response Questions

Brief Constructed Response

1   The two triangles below are similar.

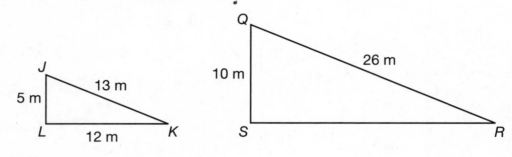

Part A   What is the perimeter of triangle *QRS*?

Part B   Use what you know about similar figures and perimeter to explain why your answer is correct. Use words and/or numbers to support your explanation.

Extended Constructed Response

2   A parallelogram has a base of 7 inches and a height of 5 inches.

Part A   What is the area of the parallelogram?

Part B
- Use what you know about the area of a parallelogram to explain why your answer is correct.
- Suppose you double the base and height of the parallelogram. How does the area of the larger parallelogram compare with the area of the original parallelogram? Use words and/or numbers to support your explanation.

3   A gift box in the shape of a rectangular prism is 8 inches long, 6 inches wide, and 4 inches high.

Part A   What is the surface area of the gift box?

Part B
- Use what you know about the surface area of rectangular prisms to explain why your answer is correct.
- Suppose you had to explain how to find the surface area of a rectangular prism to another student. Write a set of directions for finding the surface area of the gift box. Use words, numbers, and/or drawings in your directions to make them as clear as possible.

Statistics

In this unit you will learn about statistics. Statistics is the study of data. You are going to learn how to display data in a back-to-back stem-and-leaf plot.

You will need:

- a partner
- pencil and paper
- squares of paper with these numbers in red: 23, 28, 32, 35, 38, 42, 45, 45, 50
- squares of paper with these numbers in blue: 26, 29, 36, 39, 41, 41, 46, 51, 54
- small adhesive notes

Follow these steps:

1. This back-to-back stem-and-leaf plot shows the ages of members of the Hamilton family and Nelson families.

Hamilton Family		Nelson Family
Leaves	**Stem**	**Leaves**
7 3 1	1	0 4 5
3 2	2	1 3

   In this display, the stem represents the tens digit in a person's age and the leaves represent the ones digits. Therefore, the ages of the people in the Hamilton family are 17, 13, and 11, and 23 and 22. Likewise, the ages of the people in the Nelson family are 10, 14, and 15, and 21 and 23.

2. Copy this back-to-back stem and leaf plot. Use the whole sheet of paper so that there is plenty of vertical room in each row.

Red Numbers		Blue Numbers
Leaves	**Stem**	**Leaves**
	2	
	3	
	4	
	5	

3. Place the squares with the red and blue numbers in a bag. Draw a number. Then write its ones digit on an adhesive note and place it on the plot, using an entire sheet of paper.

4. Continue until all the numbers are drawn and recorded in the plot. Rearrange the adhesive notes in each row as needed to keep the digits in order. Compare your results with those of another pair of partners.

Think about it:

How can you organize your results so that it is easy to compare the median of each set of data?

Lesson 20

Back-to-Back Stem-and-Leaf Plots

A stem-and-leaf plot is a chart that organizes numbers so that you can see all of them and how they are spread out.

The heights of members of a school baseball team in inches are 59, 62, 64, 65, 68, 68, 70, 72, 73. These data can be organized into the stem-and-leaf plot below.

Heights of Baseball Team Members

Stem	Leaves
5	9
6	2 4 5 8 8
7	0 2 3

Key: 6 | 4 represents 64

In the plot above, the stems are the tens digits of the data, and the leaves are the ones digits.

A *back-to-back stem-and-leaf plot* shows two sets of data in one display.

Example 1

On a recent day, the school librarian recorded the amount of time students stayed in the library after school. She recorded these data for 9 girls and for 9 boys:

Time Spent in Library (in minutes)

Boys	15, 23, 25, 27, 29, 35, 35, 38, 55
Girls	5, 8, 9, 10, 12, 13, 15, 18, 27

Display these data in a back-to-back stem-and-leaf plot.

STRATEGY: Since the greatest place in any of the numbers is tens, make the tens digits the stems and the ones digits the leaves.

STEP 1: Start by making 3 columns. Place the tens digits from the data in the Stem column.

Number of Minutes Spent in Library

Boys		Girls
Leaves	Stem	Leaves
	0	
	1	
	2	
	3	
	4	
	5	

STEP 2: Place the ones digits in the Leaves columns. Make a key for the back-to-back stem-and-leaf plot.

Number of Minutes Spent in Library

Boys		Girls
Leaves	Stem	Leaves
	0	5 8 9
5	1	0 2 3 5 8
9 7 5 3	2	7
8 5 5	3	
	4	
5	5	

Key: 3 | 2 | 7 represents 23 minutes for boys and 27 minutes for girls.

SOLUTION: The back-to-back stem-and-leaf plot in Step 2 displays the librarian's data.

You can use a back-to-back stem-and-leaf plot to answer questions and compare two data sets.

Example 2

Use the back-to-back stem-and-leaf plot to answer these questions.

1. Who spent more time in the library—boys or girls?
2. What is the mode of the number of minutes boys spent at the library?
3. What is the median of the number of minutes girls spent at the library?

STRATEGY: **Look for patterns in the display.**

1. The data for boys cluster around the greater stems.

SOLUTION: **The boys spent more time in the library.**

2. The mode is the number that appears most often. Look for repeating leaves in the same row for boys.

SOLUTION: **The mode of the number of minutes boys spent in the library is 35.**

3. The median is the middle number in a set of data. Since there are 9 data numbers, start with the least and count to the middle, or fifth, number.

SOLUTION: **The median of the number of minutes girls spent in the library is 12.**

Sample Test Questions

Use this back-to-back stem-and-leaf plot for Questions 1–4.

Ages of Actors in a Play

Males Leaves	Stem	Females Leaves
	0	9
9	1	5 6 8
6	2	5 7
7 1 1	3	2
5	4	8
9 3	5	

Key: 7 | 3 | 2 represents a 37-year-old male and a 31-year-old female.

1 What does the clustering of the data suggest?

  A There are more older males than females.

  B There are more older females than males.

  C All the actors are about the same age.

  D It is impossible to draw a conclusion.

2 What is the median age of the female actors?

  A 18

  B 21.5

  C 22.5

  D 25

3 What is the mode of the ages of the male actors?

  A 31

  B 34

  C 37

  D There is no mode.

4 Suppose a 43-year-old male actor were added to the cast of the play. How would you add his age to the back-to-back stem-and-leaf plot?

  A Place a 4 in the leaves column in the row with stem 3.

  B Place a 4 and 3 in the leaves column in the row with stem 0.

  C Place a 3 in the leaves column in the row with stem 4.

  D Place a 3 in the leaves column in the row with stem 3.

Extended Constructed Response

These data show the finishing times in seconds of some seventh and eighth graders in a foot race.

Foot Race Finishing Times (in seconds)

7th Graders	57, 63, 63, 65, 68, 72, 80
8th Graders	55, 69, 70, 73, 77, 81, 82

Part A   Organize the data in a back-to-back stem-and-leaf plot.

Foot Race Finishing Times (in seconds)

7th Graders		8th Graders
Leaves	**Stem**	**Leaves**
	5	
	6	
	7	
	8	

Part B
- Use what you know about back-to-back stem-and-leaf plots to explain why your answer is correct. You may use words and/or numbers to support your explanation.
- Write two questions that could be answered by a person reading your back-to-back stem-and-leaf plot. Provide answers for your questions.

Lesson 21

Fooled by the Display of Data

Data displays can be correct and yet be misleading.

Example 1

Jay has worked for the same company for the past 5 years. He wants to convince his supervisor to give him a raise in pay. He prepared this line graph so show how little his hourly wage has increased over the past 5 years.

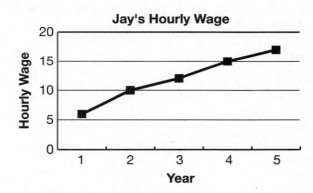

Is Jay's graph misleading? If so, how could his data be more accurately displayed?

STRATEGY: **Compare the data with the way it is displayed.**

STEP 1: Look at the axes and the scale.

Each space on the vertical axis is equal to $5, while it takes 2 spaces on the horizontal axis to equal 1 year.
The numbers on the vertical scale are very close together, making the rise of the line seem small.

STEP 2:   Redraw the graph with the numbers on the vertical scale more spread out.

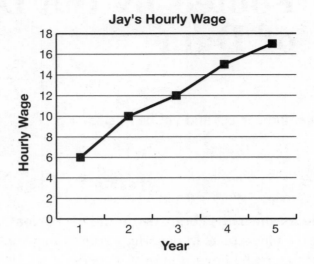

SOLUTION: The graph in Step 2 gives a fairer representation of the data.

When people conduct surveys, they try to question a group of people who are a representative sample of the population. If the sample is representative, the results will better reflect the opinions of the whole population.

Example 2

Melinda wants to conduct a telephone survey to find out if people think that the town should pay to build a new sports arena. Which of these would be the best sample to use?

   A   Her friends from her neighborhood

   B   Members of the school sports teams

   C   People who attend sports events

   D   Every tenth name in the telephone directory

STRATEGY: **Check for clues that indicate that the sample may not be representative.**

CHOICE A: People who are her friends may not be a large enough group to be representative, and because they are in her neighborhood, they may not reflect the opinions of people in other parts of the town.

CHOICE B: Most members of sports teams would be likely to favor the arena, so this sample would not be representative.

CHOICE C: As with sports team members, people who attend sports events would be likely to favor the arena.

CHOICE D: This method is random. People who are in favor are as likely to be contacted as people who are not.

SOLUTION: **The best sample for Melinda to use would be every tenth name in the telephone directory—choice D.**

Sample Test Questions

1 This bar graph shows the results of a survey that asked seventh-grade students where they wanted to go for a field trip.

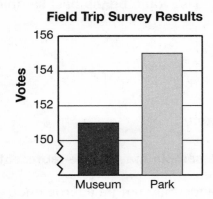

Field Trip Survey Results

What can you conclude from this bar graph?

A Three times as many students voted for the park as for the museum.

B Three times as many students voted for the museum as for the park.

C Four more people voted for the museum than for the park.

D Four more people voted for the park than for the museum.

2 This line graph shows the change in average normal temperature in Baltimore from January through April.

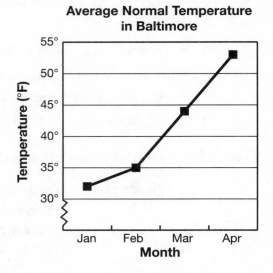

Average Normal Temperature in Baltimore

What can you conclude from this line graph?

A It is colder in December than in January.

B The degree temperature is almost twice as high in February than it is in January.

C It is about 10° warmer in March than in February.

D The degree temperature is four times higher in March than in January.

3 Bill wants to survey students in his school to find out what they think about the cafeteria food. Which group would be a representative sample of the population of the whole school?

A Students who eat the cafeteria food every day

B Students who bring their lunch to school every day

C Every tenth student who enters the school building in the morning

D Students with whom Bill eats lunch every day

4 Karen would like to collect data on what people think about laws that would restrict cell phone use. Which group of people would be a representative sample?

A People who own cell phones

B People who do not own cell phones

C People chosen at random at the mall

D Working parents

Brief Constructed Response

This graph shows the results of an election for class president.

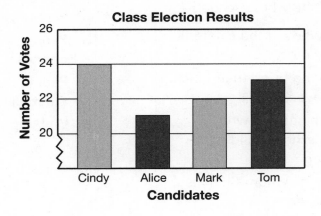

Part A   Write a conclusion that you can draw from this graph about how Alice's votes compared with Tom's votes.

Part B   Use what you know about data displays that can be misleading to explain why your answer is correct. Use words and/or numbers to support your explanation.

Lesson 22

Which Measure is the Best?

Three measures of central tendency you have studied are the mean, the median, and the mode.

The **mean** is the sum of the numbers in a set of data divided by the number of data items.

The **median** is the middle number in a set of data when the data are arranged in order. If there are two middle numbers, the median is the average of the two middle numbers.

The **mode** is the number that appears most often in a set of data. A set of data may have no mode, one mode, or more than one mode.

Sometimes one measure of central tendency is better than another for describing a set of data.

Example 1

These are the daily salaries of 7 people who work for the same company:

$76, $94, $88, $256, $90, $95, and $92.

Which measure of central tendency best describes the typical daily salary?

STRATEGY: **Find each measure and compare it with the data set.**

STEP 1: Find the mean.

$$\text{mean} = \frac{76 + 94 + 88 + 256 + 90 + 95 + 92}{7} = \frac{791}{7} = 113$$

The mean is greater than 6 of the 7 salaries, so it is not the best measure.

STEP 2: Find the median.

Arrange the data in numerical order:
76, 88, 90, 92, 94, 95, 256

The median is the middle number, 92.
The median is close to many of the numbers in the data set.

STEP 3:   Find the mode.

Since no numbers are repeated in this set, there is no mode.

SOLUTION: **The median is the best measure to describe the data.**

Sometimes, more than one of the measures of central tendency can give a good description of the data.

Example 2

These are the ages of 7 people who auditioned for a role in a play:

17, 20, 22, 12, 15, 12, 21

Which measure of central tendency best describes the typical age of a person who auditioned?

STRATEGY: **Find each measure and compare it with the data set.**

STEP 1:   Find the mean.

$$\text{mean} = \frac{17 + 20 + 22 + 12 + 15 + 12 + 21}{7} = 17$$

The mean is close to many of the numbers in the set.

STEP 2:   Find the median.

Arrange the data in order:
12, 12, 15, 17, 20, 21, 22

The median is 17, the same as the mean.

STEP 3:   Find the mode.

The mode is 12. This is the least number in the data set, and it is not as close as 17 is to the other data.

SOLUTION: **Both the mean and median give equally good descriptions of the data.**

Sample Test Questions

1 These data are the inches of rainfall in a city for seven consecutive days.

0.1, 0.3, 0.0, 1.1, 0.4, 0.0, 0.2

Which measure of central tendency best describes the average daily rainfall for this period?

A   the mode only

B   the mode and the median

C   the mean and the mode

D   the mean and the median

For Questions 2–4, name the measure of central tendency that best describes the data.

2 55, 30, 21, 36, 35, 34, 55

A   the mode only

B   mode and median

C   mean and mode

D   the median only

3 43, 46, 45, 47, 45, 44

A   the mode only

B   the mean only

C   the median only

D   the mean, median, and mode

4 15, 4, 1, 3, 6, 15, 36, 5, 32

A   the median only

B   the mean and the mode

C   the median and the mean

D   the median and the mode

Brief Constructed Response

These numbers represent the amounts of money made by five students on a charity walk.

$88.50, $92, $17.50, $94.75, $87.25

Part A   Name the measure of central tendency that best describes these data.

Part B   Use what you know about measures of central tendency to explain why your answer is correct. Use words and/or numbers to support your explanation.

Progress Check for Lessons 20–22

Use this back-to-back stem-and-leaf plot for Questions 1 and 2.

Ages of Gymnastic Contestants

Males		Females
Leaves	Stem	Leaves
7	1	4 4 8 9
2	2	0 3
3 2 0 0	3	1
1	4	

Key: 2 | 2 | 0 represents a 22-year-old male and a 20-year-old female.

1 What does the clustering of the data suggest?

A There were more older females than males.

B There were more older males than females.

C All the contestants were about the same age.

D It is impossible to draw a conclusion.

2 What is the mode of the ages of the female contestants?

A 14

B 20

C 30

D 41

3 This bar graph shows the percent of students who voted for or against the new design for the school banner.

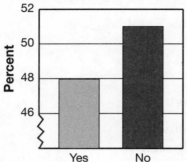

New Banner Voting Results

What can you conclude from the bar graph?

A Twice as many students voted no as voted yes.

B Three percent more voted no than yes.

C Three percent more voted yes than no.

D Half as many students voted yes as voted no.

4 Dean wants to conduct a survey to find out if people think that students spend too much time playing computer games. Which group of people would be a representative sample for him to survey?

A Parents with children in middle school

B Every twenty-fifth name in the phone directory

C Students with home computers

D People who work for computer game manufacturers

5 Which measure of central tendency best describes these data?

100, 5, 90, 95, 100

A the mode only

B the mean and the median

C the mean only

D the median only

Constructed Response Questions

Brief Constructed Response

1 These data are the heights in inches of students in a high school class.

Males	58, 59, 60, 63, 63, 64, 67, 68, 72
Females	56, 58, 62, 62, 64, 64, 65, 68, 70

Marty made this back-to-back stem-and-leaf plot to display the data in the table above.

Heights of Students in a High School Class

Males		Females
Leaves	**Stem**	**Leaves**
9 8	5	6 8
8 7 4 3 3	6	2 2 4 4 5 8
2	7	

Key: 8 | 5 | 6 represents a 58-in. tall male and a 56-in. tall female.

Part A Which data items are missing in the back-to-back stem-and-leaf plot?

Part B Use what you know about making back-to-back stem-and-leaf plots to explain why your answer is correct. Use words and/or numbers to support your explanation.

2 These data show the number of kilometers run in one week by 5 members of a track team.

24, 2, 25, 27, 22

Part A Which measure of central tendency best describes the number of kilometers run by the group as a whole?

Part B Use what you know about choosing the best measure of central tendency to explain why your answer is correct. Use words and/or numbers to support your explanation.

Probability

In this unit you will learn about probability. In order to find the probability of an event, you first need to be able to determine the number of possible outcomes of the event.

You will need:

- a partner
- paper and pencil

Follow these steps:

1. Study this problem:

   There are 3 roads from Dalton to Easton, and there are 2 roads from Easton to Fairview. What is the total number of ways to get from Dalton to Fairview by way of Easton? This drawing illustrates the problem:

   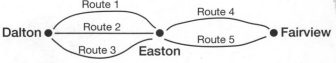

   To find the total number of ways to get from Dalton to Fairview by way of Easton, make a list:

   Dalton → Route 1 → Easton → Route 4 → Fairview
   Dalton → Route 1 → Easton → Route 5 → Fairview
   Dalton → Route 2 → Easton → Route 4 → Fairview
   Dalton → Route 2 → Easton → Route 5 → Fairview
   Dalton → Route 3 → Easton → Route 4 → Fairview
   Dalton → Route 3 → Easton → Route 5 → Fairview

   There are 6 ways to get from Dalton to Fairview by way of Easton.

2. Work with your partner to create a similar problem. Use no more than four towns in your problem. Make sure your problem has a solution.

3. Then trade problems with another pair and solve. Justify your solution with a drawing and/or a list.

Think about it:

How could you use the same method to find all the outcomes of tossing a coin and rolling a number cube?

How could you use a tree diagram to show all the possible outcomes?

Lesson 23

Outcomes of Several Independent Events

This is a special kind of die. It has the shape of a pyramid with a triangular base. It has a total of four triangular faces numbered 1 through 4.

If you perform the experiment of tossing this die, there are 4 possible outcomes: 1, 2, 3, or 4.

This spinner has three equal sectors. If you perform the experiment of spinning this spinner, there are 3 possible outcomes: A, B, or C.

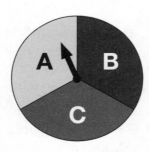

What if you performed the experiment of tossing the die *and* spinning the spinner?

Example 1

What is the total number of outcomes for spinning the spinner and tossing the die shown on the previous page?

STRATEGY: **Make a tree diagram.**

STEP 1:   List the outcomes for spinning the spinner and tossing the die.

A, or B, or C   1, or 2, or 3, or 4

STEP 2:   Use the outcomes to make a tree diagram.

Think of the experiment as spinning the spinner and then tossing the die.

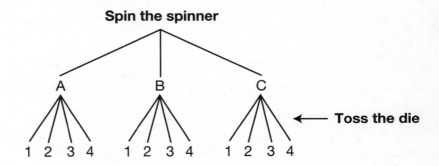

STEP 3:   Trace each path.

Start from the top of the diagram. Each path is an outcome:
A-1, A-2, A-3, A-4, B-1, B-2, B-3, B-4, C-1, C-2, C-3, C-4

SOLUTION: **There are 12 outcomes for the experiment.**

Example 2

What is the total number of outcomes for tossing a nickel, a dime, and a quarter?

STRATEGY: **Make a tree diagram.**

  STEP 1:   List the outcome for tossing each coin.

  Use H for heads and T for tails.
  Nickel: H or T
  Dime: H or T
  Quarter: H or T

  STEP 2:   Use the outcomes to make a tree diagram.

  Think of the experiment as tossing the nickel, then tossing the dime, and then tossing the quarter.

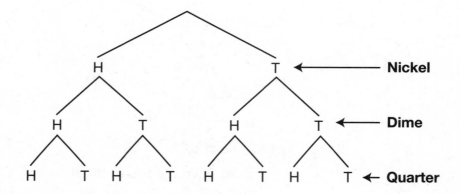

  STEP 3:   Trace each path.

  Each path is an outcome:
  H-H-H, H-H-T, H-T-H, H-T-T, T-H-H, T-H-T, T-T-H, T-T-T

SOLUTION: **There are 8 outcomes for the experiment.**

Sample Test Questions

For Questions 1–4, find the total number of outcomes for the given experiment.

1 Spinning this spinner and tossing this coin:

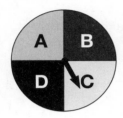

A 4

B 6

C 8

D 16

2 Rolling a number cube with faces numbered 1 through 6 and tossing a dime.

A 6

B 12

C 18

D 36

3 Tossing a penny, rolling a number cube, and spinning this spinner.

A 6

B 12

C 24

D 48

4 Tossing a dime, rolling a number cube, and drawing a card from a deck of 5 cards labeled A, B, C, D, and E.

Brief Constructed Response

Valerie designed an experiment consisting of rolling a number cube with faces numbered 1 through 6, tossing a penny, and tossing a nickel.

Part A   What is the total number of outcomes for Valerie's experiment?

Part B   Use what you know about finding outcomes to explain why your answer is correct. Use words, numbers, and/or diagrams to support your explanation.

Standard 5.B.1.a

Lesson 24
Probability of Several Independent Events

Probability is a way to measure the chance that an event will occur. You can use this ratio to find the probability, p, of an event:

$$p = \frac{\text{number of favorable outcomes}}{\text{number of possible oucomes}}$$

Two events are independent when the outcome of one event has no effect on the outcome of another event. For example,

Event 1: tossing a coin and getting tails

Event 2: tossing a number cube and getting an even number.

When finding the probability of two independent events, multiply the probabilities of the two events to get the total probability. This is called the multiplication rule.

Example 1

Find the probability of tossing a coin and getting tails and tossing a number cube and getting an even number.

STRATEGY: **Find the probability of each event and apply the multiplication rule.**

STEP 1: Find the probability of each event.

Tossing the coin:

Probability of tails $= \frac{\text{number of favorable outcomes}}{\text{number of possible oucomes}} = \frac{1}{2}$

Tossing the number cube:

Probability of even number $= \frac{\text{number of favorable outcomes}}{\text{number of possible oucomes}}$
$= \frac{3}{6} = \frac{1}{2}$

STEP 2: Apply the multiplication rule.

Probability of tails $\times$ Probability of even number

$= \frac{1}{2} \times \frac{1}{2} = \frac{1}{4}$

SOLUTION: **The probability of the independent events is $\frac{1}{4}$.**

Probability ratios can also be expressed as decimals or percents.

Example 2

Jack heard the weather forecast on TV: the probability of rain today is 20% and the probability of rain tomorrow is 50%. What is the probability that it will rain on both days?

STRATEGY: **Use the multiplication rule.**

STEP 1: Change the probabilities to fractions.

$$20\% = 0.20 = \frac{20}{100} = \frac{1}{5}$$
$$50\% = 0.50 = \frac{50}{100} = \frac{1}{2}$$

STEP 2: Apply the multiplication rule.

$$\frac{1}{5} \times \frac{1}{2} = \frac{1}{10}$$
$$\frac{1}{10} = \frac{10}{100} = 10\%$$

SOLUTION: **The probability that it will rain on both days is 10%.**

NOTE: You could also have expressed the probability as 0.10 or $\frac{1}{10}$.

Sample Test Questions

1 What is the probability that a "4" will appear when you toss a six-sided die?

A $\frac{1}{6}$

B $\frac{1}{4}$

C $\frac{1}{3}$

D $\frac{1}{2}$

2 Garth has 5 red tiles, 3 green tiles, and 2 blue tiles in a paper bag. If he chooses a tile at random, returns it to the bag, and then chooses a second tile, what is the probability that the two tiles will be green and blue in that order?

A 0.6

B 0.3

C 0.06

D 0.03

3 The weather forecast reports that the probability of rain today is 30% and the probability of rain tomorrow is 50%. What is the probability that it will rain on both days?

A 15%

B 20%

C 40%

D 80%

4 What is the probability of getting a number greater than 4 in two tosses of a single die?

A $\frac{1}{2}$

B $\frac{1}{3}$

C $\frac{1}{4}$

D $\frac{1}{9}$

Brief Constructed Response

Richard tossed a dime and tossed a die.

Part A   What is the probability that Richard will toss heads and toss a 6?

Part B   Use what you know about probability of independent events to explain why your answer is correct. Use words and/or numbers to support your explanation.

Lesson 25

Making Predictions

Surveys are used to gather information about a group. A part of the group is selected to represent the entire group. That part is called the sample. You use the information from a sample to make a prediction about the whole group.

Example 1

Gary took a survey of 30 seventh graders in his school to find out if they were in favor of going to school in the summer. Here are the results of his survey.

Yes	No	Not Sure
12	10	8

1) Based on these results, what is the probability that all seventh graders are in favor of summer school?

2) If there are 150 seventh graders in all in Gary's school, predict how many students are in favor of summer school.

STRATEGY: **Find the probability based on the sample and use it to make a prediction.**

STEP 1: Find the probability based on the sample.

$$P = \frac{\text{favorable outcomes}}{\text{total oucomes}} = \frac{12}{30} = \frac{2}{5}$$

STEP 2: Use the probability.

$\frac{2}{5}$ of the sample (30) were in favor of summer school.

$\frac{2}{5}$ of the total (150) should be in favor of summer school.

$\frac{2}{5} \times 150 = 60$

SOLUTION: **A good prediction of the total number of seventh graders who are in favor of summer school is 60.**

Example 2

In a survey in a certain neighborhood, 35 out of 50 people said that they approved a longer school day.

1) What is the probability that a person chosen from the sample surveyed approves a longer school day?

2) If there are 750 people in the neighborhood, predict the total number of people who would approve a longer school day.

STRATEGY: **Find the probability and use it to make a prediction.**

STEP 1:   Find the probability.

$$P = \frac{\text{favorable outcomes}}{\text{total oucomes}} = \frac{35}{50} = \frac{70}{100} = 70\%$$

STEP 2:   Use the probability.

70% of the sample (50) were in favor on a longer school day.

70% of the total (750) should be in favor of a longer school day.

70% of 750 = 0.7 × 750 = 525

SOLUTION: **A good prediction of the number of people who would favor a longer school day is 525.**

Sample Test Questions

1 Mitch surveyed 25 people in his town and learned that 8 of those people were in favor of building a new animal shelter. What is the probability that everyone in the town would favor the new animal shelter?

A 0.16

B 0.32

C 0.64

D 0.8

2 In Newton, 22 out of 40 adults surveyed said that they owned a cellular phone. If there are 300 adults living in Newton, what is a good prediction of the number of adults who own cellular phones?

A 55

B 65

C 165

D 265

3 Forty-two out of 50 students surveyed in Julie's school said that they planned to go to college. What is the probability that a person chosen at random from the 600 students in Julie's school plans to go to college?

A 32%

B 42%

C 52%

D 84%

4 Sally learned that the probability of drawing a green marble from a bag of different colored marbles was $\frac{3}{5}$. If there are 80 marbles in the bag, what is a good prediction of the number of green marbles?

Brief Constructed Response

In a school survey, 12 out of the 25 students surveyed said that they wanted the school to start an Internet club.

Part A   If there are 375 students in the school, what is a good prediction of the number of students who would want the school to start an Internet club?

Part B   Use what you know about making predictions to explain why your prediction is a good one. Use words and/or numbers to support your explanation.

Progress Check for Lessons 23–25

1 Pamela designed an experiment that consisted of tossing a nickel, tossing a number cube, and spinning a spinner with 3 equal sectors labeled A, B, C. What is the total number of outcomes for her experiment?

A 6

B 11

C 36

D 72

2 What is the probability of tossing a penny and getting tails and tossing a number cube and getting a prime number?

A 0.75

B 0.50

C 0.25

D 0.20

3 The probability of rain today is 50% and the probability of rain tomorrow is 10%. What is the probability that it will rain on both days?

A 5%

B 30%

C 40%

D 60%

4 The probability of drawing a blue marble from a bag is $\frac{2}{3}$ and the probability of spinning a blue sector on a spinner is $\frac{1}{6}$. What is the probability of drawing a blue marble and spinning blue?

A $\frac{1}{18}$

B $\frac{1}{9}$

C $\frac{2}{3}$

D $\frac{5}{6}$

5 In a survey of 50 people who live in the same town, 30 people said that they think that their mayor was doing a good job. There are 775 people in the town. What is the probability that a person chosen at random thinks that the mayor is doing a good job?

A 20%

B 40%

C 60%

D 75%

6 In a survey of 40 students, 12 said that they are planning to go to the school football game on Saturday. There are 900 students in the school. What is a good prediction of the number of students who plan to go to the game?

A 270

B 360

C 480

D 540

Constructed Response Questions

Brief Constructed Response

1 An experiment consists of spinning this spinner, tossing this 4-sided die, and tossing this coin.

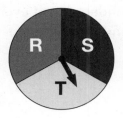 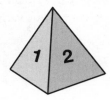

Part A How many outcomes does this experiment have?

Part B Use what you know about finding outcomes to explain why your answer is correct. Use words, numbers, and/or diagrams to support your explanation.

2   Gina has 12 red marbles, 5 green marbles, and 3 blue marbles in a paper bag.

Part A   If she chooses a marble at random, returns it to the bag, and then chooses a second marble, what is the probability that the two marbles will be red and blue in that order?

Part B   Use what you know about probability of independent events to explain why your answer is correct. Use words and/or numbers to support your explanation.

3   Twenty-eight of 40 students surveyed said that the school should expand its sports program. There are 680 students in the school.

Part A   What is a good prediction of the number of students in the school who think that the school should expand its sports program?

Part B   Use what you know about probability and making predictions to explain why your prediction is a good one. Use words and/or numbers to support your explanation.

Number Relationships and Computation

In this unit you will learn about using numbers. You can use counters to learn about operations with numbers known as integers.

You will need:

- a partner
- a collection of yellow and red counters or small squares of paper labeled (+) or (−)
- pencil and paper for recording results

Follow these steps:

1. You can use counters to show addition of integers with different signs. For example, to find the sum +5 + −7, you would collect 5 yellow (or positive) counters and 7 red (or negative) counters.

   Then pair each positive counter with a negative counter. Each pair represents +1 + −1, or 0.

   Then count the number of counters that have not been paired. Since there are two negative counters remaining, the sum is −2, or +5 + −7 = −2.

2. Take a small handful of counters. While your partner watches, arrange the tiles to find the sum represented by the tiles. Have your partner record the number of positive counters, the number of negative counters, and the result. For example, if you had 17 positive counters and 13 negative counters, your partner would record +17 + −13 = +4.

3. Switch roles until each of you has found at least two sums using the counters.

Think about it:

Suppose that there are no tiles remaining after the positive and negative counters have all been paired. What is the sum?

What shortcut could you use to find the sum of integers without using counters?

How could you use counters to show subtraction, such as −7 − (−5)?

Lesson

26 Exponents

This lesson develops several rules for working with exponents.

6^3 stands for $6 \times 6 \times 6$, or in standard form, 216.

For 6^3, the number 6 is called the base, and 3 is the exponent of 6.

6^3 can be read as 6 **to the third power**, or 6 **cubed**.

Example 1

Write $(-7)^3$ as a standard numeral.

STRATEGY: **Show the complete multiplication and do the math.**

STEP 1: Show the multiplication.

$(-7)^3 = -7 \times -7 \times -7$

STEP 2: Do the math.

$(-7 \times -7) \times -7 = (49) \times -7 = -343$

SOLUTION: $(-7)^3 = -343$.

162

Example 2

Find the missing exponent n: $3^3 \times 3^4 = 3^n$

STRATEGY: **Show the complete multiplication.**

STEP 1: Write out the multiplication for 3^3.

$3^3 = 3 \times 3 \times 3$

STEP 2: Write out the multiplication for 3^4.

$3^4 = 3 \times 3 \times 3 \times 3$

STEP 3: Write out the full multiplication for $3^3 \times 3^4$.

$3^3 \times 3^4 = (3 \times 3 \times 3) \times (3 \times 3 \times 3 \times 3)$

STEP 4: Write the full multiplication in exponent form.

$(3 \times 3 \times 3) \times (3 \times 3 \times 3 \times 3) = 3^7$

SOLUTION: $3^3 \times 3^4 = 3^7$, so $n = 7$

Example 2 illustrates this rule:

Rule 1: $a^s \times a^t = a^{s+t}$ for any number a and for integers s and t.

The rule says: add the exponents when multiplying two numbers in exponent form with the same base.

Example 3

Find the missing exponent n: $(4^2)^3 = 4^n$

STRATEGY: **Write the full multiplication for the outer exponent.**

STEP 1: Write the full multiplication for the exponent 3 of $(4^2)^3$.

$$(4^2)^3 = 4^2 \times 4^2 \times 4^2$$

STEP 2: Use Rule 1.

$$4^2 \times 4^2 \times 4^2 = 4^6$$

SOLUTION: $(4^2)^3 = 4^6$, so $n = 6$.

Example 3 illustrates this rule:

Rule 2: $(a^s)^t = a^{st}$ for any number a and for any integers s and t.

This rule says: multiply the exponents when raising a number with an exponent to a power.

Here is another rule you need to know.

Rule 3: $\dfrac{a^s}{a^t} = a^{s-t}$ where a is any number and s and t are integers.

This rule says: subtract the exponents when dividing two numbers in exponent form with the same base.

Example 4

Find n for $\dfrac{6^5}{6^2} = 6^n$

STRATEGY: **Use Rule 3.**

$$\frac{6^5}{6^2} = 6^{5-2} = 6^3$$

SOLUTION: $n = 3$

Sample Test Questions

1 $8^3 = ?$

    A   11   **C**   64

    B   24   **D**   512

2 $(-9)^2$

    A   −81   **C**   18

    B   −18   **D**   81

3 $2^3 \times 3^3$

    A   35   **C**   125

    B   54   **D**   216

4 $9^2 \times 9^1 = ?$

    A 9^1 **C** 9^3

    B 9^2 **D** 9^4

5 $(2^3)^3 = ?$

    A 2^3 **C** 2^9

    B 2^6 **D** 2^{27}

6 $(4^3)^4 = ?$

    A 4^1 **C** 4^{12}

    B 4^7 **D** 4^{16}

7 $7^5 \div 7^2 = ?$

    A 7^3 **C** 7^{10}

    B 7^7 **D** 7^{25}

8   Find n: $(5^2)^4 = 5^n$

    A   8   **C**   4

    B   6   **D**   2

9   Find n: $10^7 \div 10^1 = 10^n$

    A   6   **C**   8

    B   7   **D**   10

10   Write 9^3 as a standard numeral.

Brief Constructed Response

Tim used the numerals 2, 3, and 5 to write this expression:

$2^3 \times 2^5$

Part A   Write an expression equivalent to Tim's expression using the base 2 and just one exponent.

Part B   Use what you know about expressions with exponents to explain why your answer is correct. Use words and/or numbers to support your explanation.

Lesson 27

Square Roots

This lesson is about taking the square root—the opposite of squaring numbers.

You square a number when you multiply the number by itself.

To square 3, multiply $3 \times 3 = 9$, or $3^2 = 9$.

We say, "3 squared is 9."

Square numbers get their name from the square figure.

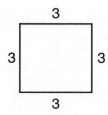

The area of this square is 3×3, or 3^2, or 3 squared.

The opposite, or inverse, of squaring a number is taking the square root.

The square root of 9 is 3, since $3^2 = 9$.

The symbol for square root is $\sqrt{}$

We write $\sqrt{9} = 3$.

Example

Find $\sqrt{36}$.

STRATEGY: **Think of a number that when squared equals 36.**

$6^2 = 36$

SOLUTION: $\sqrt{36} = 6$

Sample Test Questions

1 Find $\sqrt{25}$.

  A 5

  B 12.5

  C 50

  D 625

2 Find $\sqrt{100}$.

  A 50

  B 25

  C 10

  D 1

3 Find $\sqrt{64}$.

  A 2

  B 4

  C 8

  D 32

4 Find $\sqrt{81}$.

  A 81

  B 40.5

  C 18

  D 9

Brief Constructed Response

The area of a square is 49 square units. Diane wrote this expression to find the length of one side of the square:

$\sqrt{49}$

Part A Find the length of one side of the square.

Part B Use what you know about finding the square root to explain why your answer is correct. Use words and/or numbers to support your explanation.

Lesson 28

Decimals in Expanded Notation

A place-value chart is useful for reading and understanding decimals.

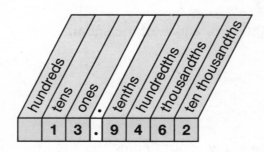

You can write the decimal as 13.9462.

You can also write the decimal as a sum in expanded notation using the place value of each digit:

1 ten + 3 ones + 9 tenths + 4 hundredths + 6 thousandths + 2 ten thousandths

10 + 3 + 0.9 + 0.04 + 0.006 + 0.0002

Example 1

Write this number in expanded notation:

5.603

STRATEGY: **Use the value of each digit to write a sum.**

5 + 0.6 + 0.00 + 0.003

Since there are no hundredths and the value of 0.00 is 0, you can leave 0.00 out of the sum.

SOLUTION: **In expanded notation, 5.603 is 5 + 0.6 + 0.003.**

Example 2

Write the following in standard form.

9 + 0.04 + 0.0008

STRATEGY: **Find the sum.**

Keep the decimal points aligned.

```
    9.0
    0.04
+   0.0008
─────────
    9.0408
```

SOLUTION: **The standard form for 9 + 0.04 + 0.0008 is 9.0408.**

Sample Test Questions

1 What is 2.345 in expanded notation?

A 2000 + 300 + 40 + 5
B 0.2 + 0.03 + 0.004 + 0.0005
C 2 + 0.3 + 0.04 + 0.005
D 2 + 0.3 + 0.004 + 0.0005

2 What is 10.2035 in expanded notation?

A 1 + 0.2 + 0.003 + 0.0005
B 1 + 0 + 0.2 + 0.003 + 0.0005
C 10 + 0.2 + 0.03 + 0.005
D 10 + 0.2 + 0.003 + 0.0005

3 What is the standard notation for the following?

30 + 0.5 + 0.0006

A 3.5006
B 30.5006
C 30.506
D 30.56

4 What is the standard notation for the following?

4 + 0.07 + 0.005

Brief Constructed Response

The population density of a state is found by dividing the population by the land area. In the year 2000, the population density of Maryland was 541.895.

Part A   Write the population density of Maryland in expanded notation.

Part B   Use what you know about writing decimals in expanded notation to explain why your answer is correct. Use words and/or numbers to support your explanation.

Lesson 29

Equivalent Rational Numbers

A positive rational number is any number that can be expressed as the ratio of two whole numbers, excluding zero in the second term.

A rational number may have the form of a fraction, decimal, or percent. You should know how to change one form to another equivalent form.

A good way to change fractions to percents is to first change fractions to decimals.

This table will help with the more common fractions.

Fraction-Decimal Equivalents

Fraction		Decimal
$\frac{1}{10}$	=	0.1
$\frac{1}{8}$	=	0.125
$\frac{1}{5}$	=	0.2
$\frac{1}{4}$	=	0.25
$\frac{1}{3}$	=	0.333... or $0.\overline{3}$
$\frac{1}{2}$	=	0.5

From this chart you can find other common equivalents. For example, to find the decimal equivalent for $\frac{3}{8}$, multiply the decimal equivalent for $\frac{1}{8}$ by 3:

$$\frac{3}{8} = 3 \times \frac{1}{8} = 3 \times 0.125 = 0.375$$

Example 1

Change the fraction $\frac{3}{5}$ to a decimal.

STRATEGY: **Use the table.**

STEP 1: Find the decimal equivalent for $\frac{1}{5}$.

$$\frac{1}{5} = 0.2$$

STEP 2: Multiply the decimal equivalent for $\frac{1}{5}$ by 3.

$$\frac{3}{5} = 3 \times \frac{1}{5} = 3 \times 0.2 = 0.6$$

SOLUTION: **The decimal equivalent for $\frac{3}{5}$ is 0.6.**

Example 2

Change the decimal 0.12 to a fraction.

STRATEGY: **Use the place value in the decimal to write a fraction.**

STEP 1: Use the place value.

0.12 is twelve hundredths, or $\frac{12}{100}$.

STEP 2: Express the fraction in lowest terms.

$$\frac{12}{100} = \frac{3}{25}$$

SOLUTION: **The fraction equivalent of 0.12 is $\frac{3}{25}$.**

Example 3

Change $\frac{5}{8}$ to a percent.

STRATEGY: **First change the fraction to a decimal.**

STEP 1: Change $\frac{5}{8}$ to a decimal.

Since $\frac{1}{8} = 0.125$, then $\frac{5}{8} = 5 \times 0.125 = 0.625$.

STEP 2: Change the decimal 0.625 to a percent.

To change a decimal to a percent, move the decimal point two places to the right. This is the same as multiplying by 100.
$0.625 = 62.5\%$

SOLUTION: **The percent equivalent to $\frac{5}{8}$ is 62.5%.**

Example 4

Change $\frac{4}{9}$ to a percent.

STRATEGY: **First change the fraction to a decimal.**

    STEP 1:   Change $\frac{4}{9}$ to a decimal.

                  Divide 4 by 9.

                  $4 \div 9 = 0.444...$ or $0.\overline{4}$

    STEP 2:   Change the decimal to a percent.

                  $0.444... = 44.\overline{4}\%$

SOLUTION: **The percent equivalent of $\frac{4}{9}$ is $44.\overline{4}\%$ or 44.4% when rounded to the nearest tenth of a percent.**

Example 5

Express 6% as a decimal.

STRATEGY: **Use the meaning of percent.**

Percent means hundredths, so 6% is 6 hundredths, or 0.06.

Another way to change a percent to a decimal is to move the decimal point two places to the left.

SOLUTION: **The decimal equivalent of 6% is 0.06.**

Example 6

Express 250% as a fraction.

STRATEGY: **Use the meaning of percent.**

    STEP 1:   Use the meaning of percent.

                  Percent means hundredths, so write 250 over 100.

                  $\frac{250}{100}$

    STEP 2:   Express the fraction in lowest terms.

                  $\frac{250}{100} = 2 + \frac{50}{100} = 2 + \frac{1}{2} = 2\frac{1}{2}$.

SOLUTION: **The fraction equivalent of 250% is the mixed number $2\frac{1}{2}$.**

Sample Test Questions

For Questions 1 and 2, find the decimal equivalent for each fraction.

1 $\frac{7}{8} = ?$

    A   0.125

    B   0.675

    C   0.775

    D   0.875

2 $\frac{7}{20} = ?$

    A   35

    B   3.5

    C   0.35

    D   0.035

For Questions 3–5, find the percent equivalent of each fraction.

3 $\frac{3}{4} = ?$

    A   75%

    B   34%

    C   7.5%

    D   0.75%

4 $\frac{3}{7} = ?$

    (Answer to the nearest tenth)

    A   42.8%

    B   42.9%

    C   4.28%

    D   4.29%

5 $\frac{7}{4} = ?$

    A   0.175%

    B   1.75%

    C   17.5%

    D   175%

6 What is the fraction equivalent of 0.08?

A $\frac{2}{25}$

B $\frac{1}{8}$

C $\frac{1}{5}$

D $\frac{4}{5}$

7 What is the percent equivalent of 0.96?

A 0.0096%

B 9.6%

C 96%

D 9600%

8 What is the decimal equivalent of 100%?

A 0.01

B 0.1

C 1.0

D 10

9 What is the fraction equivalent of 45%?

A $\frac{9}{25}$

B $\frac{1}{5}$

C $\frac{9}{20}$

D $\frac{4}{5}$

Brief Constructed Response

On a school field trip $\frac{11}{20}$ of the students were boys.

Part A   What is the percent equivalent to $\frac{11}{20}$?

Part B   Use what you know about equivalent rational numbers to explain why your answer is correct. Use words and/or numbers to support your explanation.

Lesson 30

Comparing and Ordering Rational Numbers

Integers are 0, 1, −1, 2, −2, 3, −3, and so forth.

Rational numbers are numbers that can be expressed as fractions that can be formed from integers. For example, $\frac{6}{7}$, $\frac{-3}{13}$, $\frac{3}{-4}$ are all rational numbers. Rational numbers include all decimals with a finite number of digits (0.5, 1.3652, and 4.0007) or repeating patterns (0.143143143. . . and $3.\overline{67}$). Rational numbers also include all percents that can be expressed as rational-number decimals.

One of the best ways to compare rational numbers is to write them as decimals.

Example 1

Which rational number is greater, $\frac{2}{3}$ or 0.6767?

STRATEGY: **Write the fraction as a decimal and compare the numbers as decimals.**

STEP 1: Find the decimal equivalent of $\frac{2}{3}$.

If you do not know the decimal equivalent of $\frac{2}{3}$, then use your calculator.

$$\boxed{2} \;\boxed{\div}\; \boxed{3} \;\boxed{=}\; 0.6666666$$

In your calculator window, this decimal will end after 7 or more digits, but the decimal is an infinite decimal of 6's. (Sometimes, you will see a 7 at the end of the 6's, if your calculator rounds off the last place it shows.)
$\frac{2}{3} = 0.6666...$

STEP 2: Compare the two decimals.

0.6767 > 0.6666..., since the digit (7) in the hundredths place of 0.6767 is greater than the digit (6) in the hundredths place of 0.6666...

SOLUTION: $0.6767 > \frac{2}{3}$

Example 2

Place these numbers in order from least to greatest: $5\frac{1}{6}$, 5.16, 5.16% and $5.\overline{16}$.

STRATEGY: **Compare the numbers as decimals.**

STEP 1: Use your calculator to write $5\frac{1}{6}$ as a decimal.

$$\boxed{1} \; \boxed{\div} \; \boxed{6} \; \boxed{+} \; \boxed{5} \; \boxed{=} \quad 5.16666..., \text{ or } 5.1\overline{6}$$

STEP 2: Write 5.16% as a decimal.

Move the decimal point two places to the left.
5.16% = 0.0516

STEP 3: Write out 4 places of $5.\overline{16}$.

The symbol $.\overline{16}$ means that the digits 1 and 6 keep repeating. Therefore, 5.16 is a repeating decimal.
$5.\overline{16}$ = 5.1616...

STEP 4: Compare the four numbers.

5.16% is the least number.

The other three numbers all have the same whole number (5), the same number in the tenths place (1), and the same number in the hundredths place (6).

The number 5.16 can be written as 5.160. Its thousandths place is 0.

Comparing the digits in the thousandths places of the three numbers shows that 5.16 is the smallest, 5.16<u>1</u>6.... is the middle number, and 5.16<u>6</u>6... is the largest.

SOLUTION: **The order of the numbers from least to greatest is 5.16%, 5.16, $5.\overline{16}$, and $5\frac{1}{6}$.**

Example 3

Place these numbers in order from greatest to least:

-9, 90%, $\frac{9}{60}$, and 9.6012

STRATEGY: **Compare the numbers as decimals.**

STEP 1:   Write 90% as a decimal.

90% = 0.9

STEP 2:   Write $\frac{9}{60}$ as a decimal.

$\frac{9}{60} = \frac{3}{20} = \frac{15}{100} = 0.15$

STEP 3:   Compare the four numbers.

Since -9 is the only negative number, it is the least of the numbers.

$0.9 > 0.15$, so $90\% > \frac{9}{60}$

Since 9.6012 is the only number greater than 1, it is the greatest of the numbers.

SOLUTION: **The order of the numbers from greatest to least is 9.6012, 90%, $\frac{9}{60}$, and -9.**

Sample Test Questions

1 Which is smaller, 0.167 or $\frac{1}{6}$, and why?

A $\frac{1}{6}$ is smaller because it has a smaller digit in the hundredths place than 0.167.

B 0.167 is smaller because it has a smaller digit in the hundredths place than $\frac{1}{6}$.

C $\frac{1}{6}$ is smaller because it has a smaller digit in the thousandths place than 0.167.

D 0.167 is smaller because it has a smaller digit in the thousandths place than $\frac{1}{6}$.

2 Choose the smallest of these numbers.

A $0.\overline{12}$

B 10%

C $\frac{4}{25}$

D 0.12

3 Choose the largest of these numbers.

A 0.78

B $-0.\overline{7}$

C 780%

D $\frac{17}{20}$

4 Place these numbers in order from least to greatest.

$$\frac{5}{12}, \frac{2}{5}, 0.4222, 42.5\%$$

A $\frac{2}{5}, \frac{5}{12}, 0.4222, 42.5\%$

B $\frac{5}{12}, \frac{2}{5}, 0.4222, 42.5\%$

C $\frac{2}{5}, 0.4222, \frac{5}{12}, 42.5\%$

D $42.5\%, 0.4222, \frac{5}{12}, \frac{2}{5}$

5 Place these numbers in order from least to greatest.

$$79\%, -7\frac{7}{30}, -6, -7\frac{11}{50}$$

A $-6, -7\frac{11}{50}, -7\frac{7}{30}, 79\%$

B $-7\frac{7}{30}, -7\frac{11}{50}, -6, 79\%$

C $79\%, -6, -7\frac{11}{50}, -7\frac{7}{30}$

D $79\%, -7\frac{7}{30}, -7\frac{11}{50}, -6$

183

Brief Constructed Response

These numbers represent math averages of four students:

$$82.8 \qquad 82\frac{4}{5} \qquad 82.802 \qquad 82\frac{48}{150}$$

Part A   Which is the highest average?

Part B   Use what you know about comparing rational numbers to explain why your answer is correct. Use words and/or numbers to support your explanation.

Progress Check for Lessons 26–30

1 $7^3 = ?$

   A 10

   B 21

   C 49

   D 343

2 $3^2 \times 4^3 = ?$

   A 72

   B 108

   C 384

   D 576

3 Find n: $7^3 \times 7^3 = 7^n$

   A 0

   B 3

   C 6

   D 9

4 Find n: $(5^3)^2 = 5^n$

   A 1

   B 5

   C 6

   D 9

5 $\dfrac{4^5}{4^2} = ?$

   A 4^3

   B 4^7

   C 4^{10}

   D 4^{25}

6 $\sqrt{16} = ?$

   A 4

   B 8

   C 32

   D 256

7 What is 27.5024 in expanded notation?

   A $20 + 7 + 0.5 + 0.02 + 0.004$

   B $20 + 7 + 0.05 + 0.002 + 0.0004$

   C $20 + 7 + 0.5 + 0.02 + 0.0004$

   D $20 + 7 + 0.5 + 0.002 + 0.0004$

8 What is $\dfrac{9}{20}$ as a percent?

   A 18%

   B 27%

   C 45%

   D 81%

9 What is a fraction equivalent of 35%?

A $\frac{3}{5}$

B $\frac{7}{10}$

C $\frac{7}{20}$

D $\frac{7}{25}$

10 Place these numbers in order from least to greatest.

$\frac{5}{6}$, 0.79, 81%, $\frac{41}{50}$

A $\frac{5}{6}$, $\frac{41}{50}$, 81%, 0.79

B 0.79, $\frac{41}{50}$, 81%, $\frac{5}{6}$

C 0.79, $\frac{5}{6}$, 81%, $\frac{41}{50}$

D 0.79, 81%, $\frac{41}{50}$, $\frac{5}{6}$

11 $2^3 \times 7^2 = ?$

Constructed Response Questions

Extended Constructed Response

1   Josh used this expression to find the area of a square with a side length of $\sqrt{5}$ inches:

$$(\sqrt{5})^2$$

Part A   Find the value of the expression $(\sqrt{5})^2$.

Part B
- Use what you know about square roots and exponents to explain why your answer is correct. Use words and/or numbers to support your explanation.
- If x is a positive number, $(\sqrt{x})^2 = x$. Explain why this is true if x is any whole number. Use words and/or numbers to support your explanation.

Brief Constructed Response

2   Two different students came up with these answers to a math problem:

$$76\frac{7}{15} \qquad 76.45$$

Part A   Which number is the greater number?

Part B   Use what you know about comparing rational numbers to explain why your answer is correct. Use words and/or numbers to support your explanation.

3   1 yard = 0.9144 meter

Part A   Write 0.9144 in expanded form.

Part B   Use what you know about expanded form of decimals to explain why your answer is correct. Use words and/or numbers to support your explanation.

188

Lesson

31

Addition, Subtraction, Multiplication, and Division of Integers

Learn the rules for the four basic operations with integers.

Rules for Adding Two Integers

- If the numbers have the same sign, add the numbers and use the sign for the sum.

- If the numbers have different signs, find the difference of the absolute values. Use the sign of the number with the greater absolute value in the answer.

Example 1

$6 + (-14)$

STRATEGY: Follow the rule for adding two integers with different signs.

STEP 1: Find the absolute value of each number.

$$|6| = 6$$

$$|-14| = 14$$

STEP 2: Find the difference of the absolute values.

$$14 - 6 = 8$$

STEP 3: Use the sign of the number with the greater absolute value.

The sign of the number with the greater absolute value is negative.

SOLUTION: $6 + (-14) = -8$

Rules for Subtracting Integers

To subtract one integer from another:

1 Change the sign of the number to be subtracted ("the second number"). If the second number is positive, make it negative; if the number is negative, make it positive.

2 Add the first number to the changed second number.

In other words, to subtract, add the opposite of the number.

Example 2

Subtract: $16 - (-13) = ?$

STRATEGY: **Follow the rules for subtracting integers.**

STEP 1: Change the sign of the number to be subtracted (the second number).

(-13) becomes 13.

STEP 2: Add the first number to the changed second number.

$16 + 13 = 29$

SOLUTION: **The answer is 29.**

Rules for Multiplying Two Integers

1 Change any negative integers to positive integers.

2 Multiply the integers as positive numbers.

3 Find the sign of the product by these rules:

Rule 1: If the signs of the numbers are the same, then the product is positive.

Rule 2: If the signs of the numbers are different, then the product is negative.

Example 3

Multiply: $(-25) \times (-3) = ?$

STRATEGY: Follow the rules for multiplying integers.

STEP 1: Change negative integers to positive integers.

(-25) and (-3), become 25 and 3.

STEP 2: Multiply the integers as positive numbers.

$25 \times 3 = 75$

STEP 3: Use the rules for finding the sign of the product.

The signs of the numbers are the same, so the product is positive.

$(-) \times (-) = (+)$

SOLUTION: The answer is 75.

Rules for Dividing Integers

1 Change any negative integers to positive integers.

2 Divide the integers as positive numbers.

3 Find the sign of the quotient (the answer) by these rules:

Rule 1: If the signs of the numbers are the same, then the quotient is positive.

Rule 2: If the signs of the numbers are different, then the quotient is negative.

Note: The rules for dividing integers are similar to the rules for multiplying integers.

Example 4

Divide: $(-20) \div (5) = ?$

STRATEGY: **Follow the rules for dividing integers.**

STEP 1: Change negative integers to positive integers.
(-20) becomes 20.

STEP 2: Divide the integers as positive numbers.
$20 \div 5 = 4$

STEP 3: Use the rules for finding the sign of the quotient.
The quotient of a negative number divided by a positive number is a negative number (Rule 2).
In abbreviated form, $(-) \div (+) = (-)$

SOLUTION: **The quotient is -4.**

Sample Test Questions

1 $-6 + 10 = ?$

    A   16

    B -16

    C   4

    D -4

2 $(-3) - (-12) = ?$

    A   9

    B -9

    C   15

    D -15

3 $4 \times (-8) = ?$

    A   4

    B   12

    C -12

    D -32

4 $(-60) \div (-4) = ?$

    A   15

    B -15

    C   64

    D -64

5 $(-2) \times (-3) \times (-5) = ?$

    A   30

    B -30

    C   11

    D -11

6 $(-5) \times (7) \times (-2) = ?$

    A   14

    B -4

    C   70

    D -70

7 $44 - (-12) = ?$

    A   56

    B -56

    C   32

    D -32

8 $(-3) \times (5) \times (-4)$

Brief Constructed Response

$(-30) - (-50) = ?$

Part A   Find the difference.

Part B   Use what you know about subtracting integers to explain why your answer is correct. Use words and/or numbers to support your explanation.

Addition, Subtraction, and Multiplication of Fractions and Mixed Numbers

Lesson 32

To add or subtract fractions or mixed numbers, first find a common denominator. Then use these rules when adding and subtracting two fractions.

Sum of Two Fractions With a Common Denominator

$$\frac{\text{sum of numerators}}{\text{common denominator}} \qquad \frac{3}{5} + \frac{1}{5} = \frac{4}{5}$$

Difference of Two Fractions With a Common Denominator

$$\frac{\text{difference of numerators}}{\text{common denominator}} \qquad \frac{7}{10} - \frac{4}{10} = \frac{3}{10}$$

Example 1

Add: $\frac{1}{6} + \frac{2}{5} = ?$

STRATEGY: **Find a common denominator.**

STEP 1: Ask: What numbers do the denominators 6 and 5 divide evenly?

The numbers that 6 and 5 divide evenly are: 30, 60, 90, and so forth—these are the multiples of 30. They are called common denominators.

STEP 2: Choose the least of the common denominators.

The least common denominator is 30.

STEP 3: Change the two fractions $\frac{1}{6}$ and $\frac{2}{5}$ to equivalent fractions with 30 as a denominator.

$$\frac{1}{6} = \frac{5}{30} \text{ and } \frac{2}{5} = \frac{12}{30}$$

STEP 4: Use the rule in the lesson strategy for adding two fractions with the same denominator.

$$\frac{5}{30} + \frac{12}{30} = \frac{17}{30}$$

SOLUTION: The sum is $\frac{17}{30}$.

Example 2

Subtract: $5\frac{3}{4} - 2\frac{1}{3} = ?$

STRATEGY: **Find a common denominator.**

STEP 1: Ask: What numbers do the denominators 4 and 3 divide evenly?

The numbers that 4 and 3 divide evenly are: 12, 24, 36 and so forth—these are the multiples of 12. They are common denominators for 4 and 3.

STEP 2: Choose the least of the common denominators.

The least common denominator is 12.

STEP 3: Change $\frac{3}{4}$ and $\frac{1}{3}$ to equivalent fractions with 12 as a denominator.

$$\frac{3}{4} = \frac{9}{12} \text{ and } \frac{1}{3} = \frac{4}{12}$$

STEP 4: Set up the subtraction with denominators of 12.

$$\begin{array}{r} 5\frac{9}{12} \\ - 2\frac{4}{12} \\ \hline \end{array}$$

STEP 5: Subtract. Use the rule on the previous page to subtract the fractions, then subtract the whole numbers.

$$\begin{array}{r} 5\frac{9}{12} \\ - 2\frac{4}{12} \\ \hline 3\frac{5}{12} \end{array}$$

SOLUTION: The difference is $3\frac{5}{12}$.

196

When we use "of" with fractions, it means multiply:

$$\frac{1}{3} \text{ of } \frac{2}{5} = \frac{1}{3} \times \frac{2}{5}$$

How to Multiply Two Fractions

Step 1: Multiply the two numerators ($1 \times 2 = 2$).

Step 2: Multiply the two denominators ($3 \times 5 = 15$).

Step 3: Form this fraction from Steps 1 and 2.

$$\frac{\text{product of numerators}}{\text{product of denominators}} = \frac{2}{15}$$

Step 4: Simplify the fraction, if necessary.

Example 3

Multiply: $1\frac{1}{3} \times 21$

STRATEGY: **Use the Rule for multiplying two fractions.**

STEP 1: Change the mixed number 1.

$$1\frac{1}{3} = \frac{4}{3}$$

STEP 2: Write the whole number 21 in fractional form.

$21 = \frac{21}{1}$ (All integers can be written in fractional form by using 1 as a denominator.)

STEP 3: Multiply using the results of Steps 1 and 2. Simplify, if necessary.

$$\frac{4}{3} \times \frac{21}{1} = \frac{4 \times 21}{3 \times 1} = \frac{84}{3} = 28$$

SOLUTION: $1\frac{1}{3} \times 21 = 28$

Sample Test Questions

Choose the answer in simplest form.

1 $\frac{5}{6} - \frac{3}{6} =$

A $\frac{1}{6}$

B $\frac{1}{3}$

C $\frac{1}{2}$

D $\frac{2}{3}$

2 $\frac{3}{4} + \frac{5}{6} =$

A $1\frac{1}{10}$

B $1\frac{1}{4}$

C $1\frac{5}{12}$

D $1\frac{7}{12}$

3 $9\frac{1}{2} - 5\frac{1}{4} =$

A $4\frac{3}{4}$

B $4\frac{1}{2}$

C $4\frac{1}{4}$

D $3\frac{1}{2}$

4 $10\frac{2}{5} + 7\frac{3}{10} =$

A $17\frac{7}{10}$

B $17\frac{3}{10}$

C $3\frac{1}{10}$

D $17\frac{1}{3}$

5 $\frac{2}{3} - \frac{1}{4} =$

A $\frac{11}{12}$

B $\frac{1}{12}$

C $\frac{5}{12}$

D $\frac{3}{7}$

6 $\frac{1}{5} + 4\frac{4}{10} =$

A $5\frac{3}{5}$

B $4\frac{3}{5}$

C $4\frac{1}{6}$

D $4\frac{1}{12}$

7 $8\frac{1}{3} + \frac{5}{6} =$

A $8\frac{1}{6}$

B $8\frac{2}{3}$

C $8\frac{5}{6}$

D $9\frac{1}{6}$

8 $7 - 3\frac{3}{12} =$

A $3\frac{3}{4}$

B $3\frac{7}{8}$

C $4\frac{5}{8}$

D $4\frac{3}{8}$

9 $1\frac{3}{4} - \frac{5}{6} =$

A $\frac{1}{12}$

B $\frac{1}{6}$

C $\frac{11}{12}$

D $1\frac{11}{12}$

10 $\frac{4}{15} + 1\frac{6}{15} =$

A $1\frac{9}{15}$

B $1\frac{1}{2}$

C $1\frac{1}{5}$

D $1\frac{2}{3}$

11 Jay ate $\frac{1}{12}$ of a pie. Frank ate $\frac{5}{12}$ of the same pie. How much more pie did Frank eat?

A $\frac{1}{2}$

B $\frac{1}{3}$

C $\frac{1}{12}$

D $\frac{1}{4}$

12 Dar completed $\frac{3}{10}$ of her homework before dinner. What fraction of her homework does she still have to complete?

A $\frac{9}{10}$

B $\frac{7}{10}$

C $\frac{1}{5}$

D $\frac{3}{5}$

13 Find $\frac{1}{3}$ of $\frac{1}{4}$.

A $\frac{1}{7}$

B $\frac{1}{2}$

C $\frac{1}{12}$

D $\frac{4}{3}$

14 Multiply: $3\frac{1}{3} \times \frac{1}{2} = ?$

A 9

B $\frac{2}{3}$

C $\frac{5}{3}$

D $\frac{20}{3}$

15 Multiply: $4 \times 3\frac{1}{2} = ?$

A 14

B $\frac{9}{14}$

C $\frac{7}{3}$

D $\frac{14}{3}$

In Questions 16 and 17, simplify the expressions. Remember to use the order of operations.

16 $2 \times 1\frac{4}{5} + \frac{3}{5}$

A $\frac{21}{25}$

B 3

C $4\frac{1}{5}$

D $4\frac{4}{5}$

17 $\frac{3}{10} + \frac{4}{15} \times 2\frac{7}{10}$

A $\frac{9}{25}$

B $\frac{18}{25}$

C $\frac{4}{5}$

D $1\frac{1}{50}$

Brief Constructed Response

A scenery designer wants to cover wooden frames with fabric and then paint the frames to create scenery for a play. Each frame needs $3\frac{2}{3}$ yd of fabric.

Part A   How much fabric will the designer need to buy in order to cover 18 wooden frames?

Part B   Use what you know about operations with fractions to explain why your answer is correct. Use words and/or numbers to support your explanation.

Lesson 33

Properties of Numbers

There are a number of math rules that you need to know to do algebra problems. These rules are often called properties. You don't have to memorize their names.

Addition Properties

1. Commutative Property of Addition

Numbers can be added in any order—the sum will be the same.

$$27 + 31 = 58 \quad \text{or} \quad 31 + 27 = 58$$

2. Associative Property of Addition

Three numbers can be added in different ways—the sum is the same.

$$(17 + 13) + 9 = 30 + 9 = 39 \quad \text{or} \quad 17 + (13 + 9) = 17 + 22 = 39$$

3. Identity Property of Addition

If you add 0 to any number, the sum is that number.

$$5\frac{1}{2} + 0 = 5\frac{1}{2} \quad \text{or} \quad 0 + 5\frac{1}{2} = 5\frac{1}{2}$$

4. Additive Inverse Property

The additive inverse of a number is the opposite of that number. The sum of a number and its additive inverse is 0.

$$26 + (-26) = 0 \quad \text{or} \quad -26 + 26 = 0$$

Multiplication Properties

1. Commutative Property of Multiplication

Numbers can be multiplied in any order—the product will be the same.

$$9 \times 8 = 72 \quad \text{or} \quad 8 \times 9 = 72$$

2. Associative Property of Multiplication

Three numbers can be multiplied in any order—the product will be the same.

$$12 \times (3 \times 4) = 144 \quad \text{or} \quad (12 \times 3) \times 4 = 144$$

3. Identity Property of Multiplication

When one of two factors is 1, the product is the other factor.

$$1 \times 94 = 94 \quad \text{or} \quad 94 \times 1 = 94$$

4. Zero Property of Multiplication

When one of the factors is 0, the product is 0.

$$0 \times 62 = 0 \quad \text{or} \quad 62 \times 0 = 0$$

Multiplication and Addition Property

1. Distributive Property of Multiplication and Addition

The distributive property combines multiplication and addition. It is one of the more important properties in mathematics.

When 1 number is multiplied by the sum of 2 numbers, get the answer by first multiplying each number by the factor and *then* adding.

$$6 \times (20 + 4) = 6 \times 20 + 6 \times 4 \quad \text{[sometimes written as } (6 \times 20) + (6 \times 4)]$$

NOTE: If you see $6(20 + 4)$, it is the same as $6 \times (20 + 4)$.

Sample Test Questions

1 Which expression is the same as $(5 \times 3) \times 7$?

A $5 \times (3 + 7)$

B $5 \times (3 \times 7)$

C $5 + (3 \times 7)$

D $(5 + 3) \times 7$

2 Which expression is the same as $5(7 + 9)$?

A $5 \times 7 + 5 \times 9$

B $5 \times 7 + 9$

C $5 \times 7 + 7$

D $5 \times 7 \times 5 \times 9$

3 Which property does this example show?

$$61 + 37 = 37 + 61$$

A associative property of addition

B commutative property of addition

C distributive property

D property of 1

4 The zero property of multiplication shows that

A $64 \times 0 = 64$

B $28 + 0 = 28$

C $1 \times 76 = 76$

D $0 \times 34 = 0$

5 Which expression is the same as

$$(12 \times 13) + (12 \times 14)?$$

A $12 \times (13 + 14)$

B $12 \times (13 \times 14)$

C $(12 + 13) \times 14$

D $(12 \times 13) + 14$

6 Which of these expressions is NOT true?

A $24 + 0 = 24$

B $1 \times 87 = 87$

C $0 \times 4 = 4$

D $0 + 75 = 75 + 0$

7 Which expression is equivalent to 7(4 + 3)?

A (7 + 4) × (7 + 3)

B 11 + 10

C 7 × 4 + 7 × 3

D 28 + 3

8 Which expression is equivalent to 2(6 + 3)?

A (2 × 6) + (2 × 3)

B 2 × 6 + 3

C 8 + 5

D (2 + 6) × (2 + 3)

9 Which property does this example show?

(−56) + 56 = 0

A identity property of addition

B additive inverse property

C commutative property of addition

D associative property of addition

Brief Constructed Response

Ben wrote this equation.

$$(5 \times 9) + (5 \times 7) = 5 \times (9 + 7)$$

Part A   Which property does Ben's equation show?

Part B   Use what you know about number properties to explain why your answer is correct. Use words and/or numbers to support your explanation.

Lesson 34

Estimation With Rational Numbers

We frequently estimate when we communicate numerical information.

Example 1

Kevin had three pieces of scrap wood whose lengths were $2\frac{1}{8}$ ft, $3\frac{2}{3}$ ft and $4\frac{1}{10}$ ft. Estimate the sum of the lengths of wood.

STRATEGY: **Round each addend and add.**

> **STEP 1:** Round each addend to the nearest whole number.
>
> $2\frac{1}{8}$ becomes 2.
>
> $7\frac{5}{6}$ becomes 8.
>
> $4\frac{1}{10}$ becomes 4.
>
> **STEP 2:** Add.
>
> $2 + 8 + 4 = 14$

SOLUTION: **The sum of the lengths is about 14 ft.**

Example 2

Stephanie had $41 in her wallet. She spent $15.95 on a CD. About how much money does she have in her wallet now?

STRATEGY: **Round the numbers and subtract.**

> **STEP 1:** Round each number.
>
> $41 becomes $40.
> $15.95 becomes $16.
>
> **STEP 2:** Subtract.
>
> $40 - 16 = 24$

SOLUTION: **She has about $24 in her wallet.**

Example 3

Carla owes $985 on her computer. She has 19 more payments to make. About how much is each payment?

STRATEGY: **Round to numbers that are easy to divide.**

      STEP 1:   Round the numbers.

                 $985 becomes $1000.

                 19 becomes 20.

      STEP 2:   Divide.

                 $1000 \div 20 = 50$

SOLUTION: **Each payment is about $50.**

Example 4

Joanna figures that she saves 27 percent when she shops at the supermarket instead of at the deli. Last Thursday she spent $83 at the deli. If she had shopped at the supermarket, about how much money would she have saved?

STRATEGY: **Use rounding.**

      STEP 1:   Round the percent to the nearest 10.

                 27 percent becomes 30 percent.

      STEP 2:   Round the amount purchased to the nearest 10.

                 $83 becomes $80.

      STEP 3:   Compute the percent saved using the rounded numbers.

                 30% of 80 = $0.30 \times 80 = 24$

SOLUTION: **The amount she would have saved is *about* $24.**

Sample Test Questions

1 The fraction $\frac{7}{8}$ is closest to which number shown on the number line?

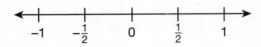

A $-\frac{1}{2}$

B   0

C $\frac{1}{2}$

D   1

2 Which would be the best way to estimate the following product?

$$34\frac{3}{22} \times 17\frac{17}{22}$$

A 34×18

B 34×17

C 35×18

D 35×17

3 Michael made 42% more money this week than last week. Last week he made $892. About how much more money did he make this week?

A $360

B $340

C $320

D $300

4 On the first day of their vacation, Corey's family drove 273 miles without stopping. What is the best estimate of their average speed if they drove for 6 hours?

A   40 miles per hour

B   45 miles per hour

C   50 miles per hour

D   55 miles per hour

5 Jodi sold 133 cans of cola at the school picnic on Saturday. She charged 80 cents for each can. What is the best estimate of how much money Jodi collected from the sale?

A $10

B $80

C $100

D $200

6 Alonzo had $79 at the start of last weekend. He spent 25% of the money. About how much did he have left?

A $20

B $40

C $50

D $60

7 Natalie bought a sweater for $29.95, a shirt for $21.85, and a cap for $12.75. What is the best estimate of the total amount she spent?

A $50

B $60

C $75

D $80

8 A theater has 789 seats. One hundred nine seats have been sold for a show. About how many seats have not been sold?

A 300

B 500

C 700

D 900

Brief Constructed Response

Jeff bought 21 sandwiches costing $4.95 each for a class party.

Part A   What is a good estimate of the total amount Jeff paid for the sandwiches?

Part B   Use what you know about estimating with rational numbers to explain why your estimate is a good one. Use words and/or numbers to support your explanation.

Lesson 35

Finding the Percent of a Total

Some questions require finding the percent of a number, such as "What percent of the students were absent last week?"

Example 1

There are 200 students in a middle school. Last week 12% of the students were absent. How many students were absent?

STRATEGY: **Change the percent to a decimal and multiply.**

>**STEP 1:** Change the percent to a decimal (see Lesson 29).
>
>Change 12% to 0.12

>**STEP 2:** Multiply by the decimal.
>
>$200 \times 0.12 = 24$

SOLUTION: **There were 24 students absent.**

Example 2

Enrico has $900 in an investment account that earns 8% interest per year. After one year, how much interest did Enrico earn?

STRATEGY: **Change the percent to a decimal and multiply.**

>**STEP 1:** Change the percent to a decimal.
>
>Change 8% to 0.08

>**STEP 2:** Multiply by the decimal.
>
>$900 \times 0.08 = 72$

SOLUTION: **Enrico earns $72 after one year.**

Example 3

A TV set is on sale for 30% off the regular price. If the regular price is $300, then what is the sale price?

STRATEGY: **Find the amount of the discount and subtract.**

STEP 1: Change the percent to a decimal.

30% is the same as 0.30

STEP 2: Find the amount of the discount.

Multiply: 0.30 × $300 = $90

STEP 3: Subtract the discount from the regular price.

$300 − $90 = $210

SOLUTION: **The sale price is $210.**

Sample Test Questions

1 Latisha's soccer team lost only 30% of its 30 games last season. How many games did they win? (There were no ties.)

A 6

B 9

C 11

D 21

2 Matt's average in math went up 20% from 75. What is the new average?

A 85

B 87

C 90

D 95

3 Keith has $750 in an investment account that earns 6% interest per year. After one year, how much interest did Keith earn?

A $4.50

B $45

C $450

D $795

4 Rosa works in an appliance store. She earns 2% commission on any appliance she sells. What will she earn if she sells an $850 refrigerator?

A $17

B $34

C $170

D $340

5 A computer monitor that regularly sells for $440 is on sale for 30% off the regular price. What is the sale price?

A $132   C $264

B $308   D $572

6 There are 640 registered voters in Mike's town. In the last election, 65% of the registered voters voted. How many people voted in the last election?

Brief Constructed Response

A leather coat that regularly sells for $165 is on sale for 40% off the regular price.

Part A   How much money will a person save who buys the coat on sale?

Part B   Use what you know about finding a percent of a total to explain why your answer is correct. Use words and/or numbers to support your explanation.

Lesson 36

Ratios and Proportions

Ratios

A ratio is the comparison of two numbers. These numbers are called the **terms** of the ratio. A ratio is often expressed as a fraction, like this: $\frac{3}{7}$. You may also see this ratio written like this: **3 : 7**. In either case, you read it as "**3 to 7**."

Example 1

Linda's team won 20 games and lost 15. What is the ratio of games won to games lost?

STRATEGY: **Write the two numbers as a fraction, and reduce if necessary.**

        STEP 1:   Write the ratio as a fraction.

                   The first term is the numerator, and the second term is the denominator: $\frac{20}{15}$ (or 20 : 15)

        STEP 2:   Reduce the fraction to lowest terms: $\frac{20}{15} = \frac{4}{3}$ (or 4 : 3)

SOLUTION: **The ratio is "4 to 3."**

        NOTE: Do NOT change a number greater than 1 to a mixed number. The ratio $\frac{4}{3}$ is NOT read as "$1\frac{1}{3}$."

                   If a fraction reduces to a whole number, then turn it into a fraction by writing 1 as the denominator—for example, $\frac{2}{1}$, or 2 to 1.

Proportions

When two ratios equal each other, the result is a proportion.

Example 2

Serena drinks 3 glasses of milk every 2 days. Write a proportion that shows how to find the number of glasses of milk she will drink in 12 days.

STRATEGY: **Set up two ratios equal to each other—one that is known and another that is unknown.**

STEP 1: Set up the first ratio comparing glasses and days.

$$\frac{3}{2}$$

STEP 2: Set up the second ratio the same way you did the first one, with n standing for the unknown number of glasses.

$$\frac{n}{12}$$

STEP 3: Write a proportion with the first ratio equal to the second ratio.

SOLUTION: $\frac{3}{2} = \frac{n}{12}$

NOTE: Make sure you set up both ratios the same way.

Once we know how to set up proportions, we need to know how to solve them.

Example 3

Solve the proportion in Example 2 to find out how many glasses of milk Serena will drink in 12 days.

STRATEGY: **Solve by cross-multiplying.**

STEP 1: We already have set up the proportion for this problem in Example 2.

$$\frac{3}{2} = \frac{n}{12}$$

STEP 2: Multiply the two numbers that are diagonally opposite each other. (This is called cross-multiplying.)

$$2n = 3 \times 12 = 36$$

STEP 3:   Solve the equation.

$$2n = 36, \text{ so } n = 18$$

SOLUTION: Serena will drink 18 glasses in 12 days.

Example 4

Sally took a survey of parents in her community. She found that 3 out of every 5 parents voted in school elections. If 450 parents are eligible to vote, how many will actually vote?

STRATEGY: Determine the proportion and cross-multiply.

STEP 1:   Find the ratio given in the problem.

The ratio expressed in this problem is "3 out of every 5 parents."
As a fraction, the ratio is:

$$\frac{\text{voting parents}}{\text{total parents}} = \frac{3}{5}$$

STEP 2:   Write the ratio for the total number of parents. Use the letter n to stand for the number of voting parents.

The ratio is:

$$\frac{\text{voting parents}}{\text{total parents}} = \frac{n}{450}$$

STEP 3:   Write the proportion using Steps 1 and 2.

$$\frac{3}{5} = \frac{n}{450}$$

STEP 4:   Cross-multiply to solve the proportion.

$$5n = 3 \times 450 = 1350$$
$$\text{So } n = 270$$

SOLUTION: 270 parents would vote out of the 450 who are eligible.

Sample Test Questions

1 Violet had 125 calories for an afternoon snack and 750 calories for lunch. What is the ratio of calories for the snack to calories for lunch?

A $\frac{1}{3}$

B $\frac{1}{4}$

C $\frac{1}{6}$

D $\frac{1}{400}$

2 Joe's Rent-a-Car rents cars at the rate of $212 for 4 days. At this rate, what would it cost to rent the same car for 10 days?

A $2120

B $583

C $530

D $520

3 Wanda's tuna salad recipe calls for 4 tablespoons of mayonnaise for every 3 lb of tuna fish. How many tablespoons of mayonnaise does she need to make 12 lb of tuna salad?

A 9

B 12

C 16

D 48

4 16 of the 24 students in Walt's class want to go to college. Use these numbers to predict the number of students who want to college if there are 552 students in the school.

A 402

B 398

C 378

D 368

5 Triangle *ABC* is similar to triangle *XYZ*. Side *AB* = 10 cm and side *XY* = 12 cm. If *XZ* = 18 cm, then *AC* = ☐?

A 12 cm

B 15 cm

C 20 cm

D 25 cm

6 Which ratio is equivalent to $\frac{48}{60}$?

A $\frac{4}{5}$

B $\frac{5}{6}$

C $\frac{7}{8}$

D $\frac{72}{90}$

Brief Constructed Response

There are 10 girls and 15 boys in Juan's class.

Part A   Express the ratio of boys to girls in simplest form.

Part B   Use what you know about ratios to explain why your answer is correct. Use words and/or numbers to support your explanation.

Lesson 37

Rates

On a trip, Gary averaged 60 miles per hour. He bought some gas for $2.00 per gallon.

60 miles per hour and $2.00 per gallon are **rates**.

A rate is a fixed ratio between two quantities of different units, like miles and hours, or dollars and gallons.

Speed is a rate. The speed of 60 miles per hour compares 60 miles to 1 hour. This rate is sometimes written as $\frac{60 \text{ miles}}{1 \text{ hour}}$.

If the second number of a rate is 1, then the rate is called a **unit rate**. 60 miles per hour is a unit rate.

Example 1

Lazlo built 30 toy airplanes in 5 hours. What is his unit rate for building toy airplanes per hour?

STRATEGY: Reduce the rate (the fraction) so that the second number (the denominator) is 1.

STEP 1: Write the rate as a fraction.

$$\frac{30 \text{ airplanes}}{5 \text{ hours}}$$

STEP 2: Divide both numerator and denominator by the denominator.

$$\frac{30 \div 5}{5 \div 5} = \frac{6}{1}$$

STEP 3: Write as a unit rate.

SOLUTION: Lazlo's unit rate was 6 toy airplanes per hour.

A common unit rate used in supermarkets is **unit price**—for example, a unit price of *35 cents per pound*. Unit prices like this enable consumers to compare prices of items that have different weights.

Example 2

18 oz of Brand X Cereal sells for $5, while 22 oz of Brand Y Cereal sells for $6. Which is the "better buy," Brand X Cereal or Brand Y Cereal?

STRATEGY: **Calculate unit prices and compare.**

STEP 1: Change Brand X Cereal to a unit price.

$\frac{5}{18} = 0.2777...$ or, to the nearest cent, 28 cents per ounce

STEP 2: Change Brand Y Cereal to a unit price.

$\frac{6}{22} = 0.2727...$ or, to the nearest cent, 27 cents per ounce

STEP 3: Compare unit prices. Which unit price is less?

The unit price for Brand Y Cereal is less than the unit price for Brand X Cereal.

SOLUTION: **Brand Y is the "better buy."**

Example 3

The train that Ernesto was on traveled 540 miles in 5 hours. What was the average speed of the train?

STRATEGY: **Use the formula for finding average speed:**

$$\textbf{Average Speed} = \frac{\textbf{total distance}}{\textbf{total time}}$$

STEP 1: Substitute in the formula above.

$$\text{Average Speed} = \frac{\text{total distance}}{\text{total time}} = \frac{540}{5}$$

STEP 2: Do the math.

$$\text{Average Speed} = \frac{540}{5} = 108$$

SOLUTION: **The average speed of the train is 108 miles per hour.**

Sample Test Questions

1   Write this price as a unit price.

$3.00 for 4 watermelons

A   60 cents per watermelon

B   75 cents per watermelon

C $1.50 for 2 watermelons

D $3.00 per watermelon

2   Write this rate as a unit rate.

45 lawns mowed in 15 days

A   3 lawns per day

B   6 lawns per 2 days

C   5 lawns per day

D   15 lawns per day

3   Victoria's family drove 672 miles in 14 hours. What was the average speed for the trip?

A   50 miles per hour

B   48 miles per hour

C   45 miles per hour

D   42 miles per hour

4   At Kenneth's school, tickets for a concert were sold at the rate of 40 per half-hour. How many tickets will be sold in 7 hours?

A   250

B   260

C   280

D   560

5   The 6 glasses of orange juice that Hector drank last week contained 360 calories. What was the unit rate? (calories per glass)

A   60

B   70

C   80

D   120

6   A carton containing 10 16-oz packages of Bahoo Gumballs sells for $29. A carton containing 20 16-oz packages of Tycos Gumballs sells for $62. Compare the unit prices for a package of gumballs.

A   Bahoo is 20 cents more.

B   Tycos is 20 cents more.

C   They sell for the same unit price.

D   It is impossible to compare unit prices.

Brief Constructed Response

Judy read a 288-page novel in 9 hours.

Part A   What was the average number of pages she read per hour?

Part B   Use what you know about rates to explain why your answer is correct. Use words and/or numbers to support your explanation.

Progress Check for Lessons 31–37

1 $54 - (-26) = ?$

    A -80

    B -28

    C 28

    D 80

2 $-44 + 35 = ?$

    A -79

    B -9

    C 9

    D 79

3 $(-12) \times (3) \times (-2) = ?$

    A -72

    B -17

    C 17

    D 72

4 $(-70) \div 5 = ?$

    A -65

    B -14

    C 14

    D 65

5 $10\frac{7}{10} - 4\frac{5}{6}$

    A $4\frac{13}{15}$

    B $5\frac{1}{2}$

    C $5\frac{13}{15}$

    D $6\frac{13}{15}$

6 $3\frac{1}{2} \times \frac{1}{3} = ?$

    A $1\frac{1}{6}$

    B $3\frac{1}{6}$

    C $3\frac{1}{5}$

    D $10\frac{1}{2}$

7   Which shows the associative property of multiplication?

    A $2(3 + 4) = 2 \times 3 + 2 \times 4$

    B $(2 \times 3) \times 4 = 2(3 \times 4)$

    C $2 \times 3 = 3 \times 2$

    D $(2 + 3) + 4 = 2 + (3 + 4)$

8 Beth made 32% more money this week than she made last week. Last week she made $694. About how much more money did she make this week?

A $180

B $210

C $240

D $280

9 A clothing store buys a coat from a manufacturer for $80. Before putting the coat up for sale, the store marks up the price by 60%. How much is the mark up?

A $14

B $20

C $48

D $140

10 Otis and Marla can decorate 16 t-shirts in 60 minutes. How many t-shirts will they be able to decorate in 90 minutes?

Constructed Response Questions

Extended Constructed Response

1   Holly said that the ratio of her allowance to Felicia's allowance is the same as the ratio of Felicia's allowance to Manny's allowance.

Part A   Write a proportion for finding Felicia's allowance.

Part B
- Use what you know about equal ratios and proportions to explain why your answer is correct. Use words and/or numbers to support your explanation.
- Suppose that Holly's allowance is $9.00 and Manny's allowance is $4.00. Use your proportion to find Felicia's allowance. Use what you know about solving proportions and finding square roots to explain why your answer is correct. Use words and/or numbers to support your explanation.

Brief Constructed Response

2 A drink contains 40% orange juice and 60% cranberry juice.

Part A What is the ratio of orange juice to cranberry juice in this drink?

Part B Use what you know about writing ratios to explain why your answer is correct. Use words and/or numbers to support your explanation.

3 A computer that regularly sells for $975 is on sale at a 40% discount.

Part A What is the sale price of the computer?

Part B Use what you know about finding a percent of a total to explain why your answer is correct. Use words and/or numbers to support your explanation.

4 At 6:00 A.M., the temperature was −7°F. By 2:00 P.M., the temperature had risen 12°.

Part A What was the temperature at 2:00 P.M.?

Part B Use what you know about operations with integers to explain why your answer is correct. Use words and/or numbers to support your explanation.

Extended Constructed Response

5   As part of her training program, Amy jogs $3\frac{1}{2}$ miles on Saturday and $2\frac{3}{4}$ miles on Sunday.

Part A   How far did she jog in all on Saturday and Sunday?

Part B
- Use what you know about mixed numbers to explain why your answer is correct. Use words and/or numbers to support your explanation.
- Amy has the goal of doubling the total distance she jogs on Saturday and Sunday. If she achieves her goal, how far will she jog on Saturday? on Sunday? on both days together? Explain why your answer is correct. Use words and/or numbers to support your explanation.

In this unit you will learn about solving problems. There are many different strategies that you can use to solve problems, but you should always follow the same basic steps.

You will need:

- a partner
- paper and pencil
- a ruler

Follow these steps:

1. Study this problem:

   - Angie, Beth, Calvin, and David are on different teams: the baseball team, the soccer team, the swimming team, and the tennis team.
   - David is the brother of the girl who is on the swimming team.
   - Angie's sport uses the largest ball.
   - Calvin's sport does not involve a bat.

   Which student plays on which team?

2. Read each clue. One way to solve this problem is to make a diagram and use reasoning to fill it in. For example, since David is the brother of the girl on the swimming team,

	Baseball	Soccer	Swimming	Tennis
Angie				
Beth				
Calvin			X	
David			X	

   you know that neither David nor Calvin is on the swimming team. Put X's in the diagram to show that David and Calvin are not on the swimming team.

   When you match a student with a sport, place an O in the chart.

3. Work with your partner to match each student with the correct sport. Compare and discuss your results with another pair of students.

Think about it:

Once you have completed the diagram, compare the information in the diagram with the given clues to check your work.

Can there be more than one solution to this problem? Explain.

Lesson

38 Using a Four-Step Method

Here is a simple four-step method to help solve problems:

STEP 1: Read the problem carefully. What are you trying to find?

STEP 2: Plan what you are going to do. What do you know? What operation should you use?

STEP 3: Carry out the plan.

STEP 4: Check your answer.

Example 1

Jeff bought 3 CDs and 1 book for $60. Each CD cost the same amount. If the book cost $12, how much did each CD cost?

STRATEGY: Follow the four-step method above.

STEP 1: Read the problem carefully.

What are you trying to find?
The cost of each CD.

STEP 2: Plan what you are going to do.

What do you know?
The cost of 3 CDs and 1 book: $60
The cost of the book: $12

What operation should you use?
First subtract the cost of the book from the total. Then divide the remaining amount by 3 to find the cost of each CD.

STEP 3: Carry out the plan.

Subtract: 60 − 12 = 48. The cost of 3 CDs is $48.
Divide: 48 ÷ 3 = 16. Each CD costs $16.

STEP 4: Check the answer.

16 × 3 = 48
48 + 12 = 60

SOLUTION: **Each CD cost $16.**

Sample Test Questions

1 Last year, Mrs. Jackson's salary was $50,239. This year, her salary is $52,085. How much more is Mrs. Jackson's salary this year?

A $1846

B $1856

C $2846

D $2856

2 A new statue 10 yards high was erected at the art museum. How many feet high is the statue?

A   2   C   30

B   20   D   33

3 Maryann spent 3 hours and 22 minutes writing her English composition. Keisha spent 2 hours and 48 minutes writing her English composition. How many fewer minutes did it take Keisha to write her English composition?

A   32   C   36

B   34   D   38

4 Ron made a long distance call for 19 minutes and was charged 43 cents for each minute of the call. What was the total charge for this call?

A $3.67   C $8.17

B $4.30   D $10.07

5 The 10 members of the debate club shared 3 key lime pies. Each pie was cut into 8 slices. If each person ate the same number of pieces, how many whole pieces did each eat?

A   1   C   3

B   2   D   4

6 The monthly charge for e-mail from the new Speedy Delivery Company is $8.00 plus $0.10 for each e-mail sent after the first 50 e-mails. If Cecilia sent 75 e-mails last month, how much did the Speedy Delivery Company charge her?

A $7.50   C $10.50

B $8.00   D $15.50

7 Matti's average after 5 quizzes is 85. What is the total number of points she got on all 5 quizzes?

233

Mario bought 2 DVDs and 3 videos. Each DVD had the same price, and each video had the same price. The total cost for the three videos was $45 before tax. His total purchase came to $81 before tax.

Part A   What was the cost of each DVD?

Part B   Use what you know about using a four-step method to solve a problem to explain why your answer is correct. Use words and/or numbers to support your explanation.

Lesson 39

Using Information and Formulating Questions

Sometimes a problem may not have enough information.

Example 1

Adele earns $10 per hour for the first 40 hours she works in a week. She earns $1\frac{1}{2}$ times her hourly pay for each hour she works over 40 hours in a week. How much did she earn last week?

What additional information do you need to solve this problem?

    A the number of days she worked last week

    B the time she arrived at work each day

    C the number of hours she worked last week

    D no additional information is needed to solve the problem.

STRATEGY: **Try to solve the problem without looking at the answer choices. Decide what additional information, if any, you need. Compare what you need with the choices.**

    Choice A: The number of days she worked will not give you the information you need: the number of hours she worked.

    Choice B: The time she arrived at work each day will not tell you the number of hours she worked.

    Choice C: This is the information you need.

    Choice D: You knew after reading the problem that some information was needed.

SOLUTION: **The answer is C.**

Sample Test Questions

1 All of these factors are normally used to determine the price of a hamburger deluxe at Fred's Burger Restaurant, except one. Which one?

   A the cost of making the hamburger

   B the number and cost of the extras

   C the number of people the restaurant can hold

   D the payroll of the employees

2 Ray's school has 18 students for each teacher, and Donna's school has 23 students for each teacher. What conclusion can you draw from this information?

   A There are more students in Ray's school than in Donna's school.

   B There are more teachers in Donna's school than in Ray's school.

   C You cannot determine which school has more teachers.

   D Ray goes to an elementary school and Donna goes to a high school.

3 A few major league baseball players are paid over 5 million dollars a year. If the season consists of 162 games and each game takes about 2.5 hours, about how much per hour would a 5-million-dollar player be paid if the player played in every game?

A $1200

B $2500

C $12,000

D $120,000

4 Teachers at the McFarland Street Middle School want to rate each student's work in social studies. Which question is the least important to ask?

A What are the results of the student's tests?

B What is the quality of the student's written work?

C How many times did the student take the textbook home?

D How many times did the student answer questions in class?

Extended Constructed Response

Charles left his house and walked for 30 minutes to Gary's house. He visited Gary for $2\frac{1}{2}$ hours. Then he walked for 20 minutes to get to the library. He stayed at the library for 1 hour. At what time did he leave the library?

Part A   What additional information, if any, do you need to solve this problem?

Part B
- Use what you know about using information in a problem to explain why your answer is correct. Use words and/or numbers to support your explanation.
- Provide information so that the problem can be solved. Then solve the problem. Explain your steps.

Lesson

40

Using Strategies to Solve Problems

This lesson explores possible strategies that you can use to solve problems that are not routine everyday problems.

When you work with non-routine problems, don't be discouraged if you don't find a solution quickly. In fact, don't be surprised if it takes time to find a successful strategy. You may have to think the problem over for a while before you can hit upon a strategy that works. You may have to change from one strategy to another before you get rolling. Keep in mind that there's usually more than one way to solve a problem.

These are some of the strategies that you can use:

Strategies

1. Act it out

2. Make a model

3. Draw a picture

4. Make a chart or graph

5. Look for a pattern

6. Solve a simpler problem

7. Make a list

8. Work backward

9. Guess and check

10. Break the problem into parts

The examples on the following pages will illustrate three of these strategies.

Example 1

You are one of 10 people invited to join a table tennis (ping pong) club. When the club first met, each new member shook hands with the other 9 new members. How many handshakes were there?

As you can see, this is not a standard problem. There are several strategies you could use to solve it. We will show one of the strategies.

STRATEGY: **Use Strategy Number 1: Act it out. We will go through the main steps of acting it out.**

STEP 1: Suppose you are the first person to shake hands. How many people do you shake hands with?

> You shake hands with 9 other members—that's 9 handshakes.

STEP 2: Jodi is the second member to shake hands with the other members. How many people does she shake hands with?

> Nine people? No, she already shook hands with you, so she shakes hands with 8 people—8 handshakes.

STEP 3: Phil is next, the third person to shake hands with the other new members. How many people does he shake hands with?

> Not 9 or 8, but 7 new members. He already shook hands with you and Jodi—7 handshakes.
> The next person in this chain shakes hands with 1 fewer persons than the person before.
> This pattern leads to this sum for the total number of handshakes:
> $9 + 8 + 7 + 6 + 5 + 4 + 3 + 2 + 1$

STEP 4: Add the string of numbers.

> $9 + 8 + 7 + 6 + 5 + 4 + 3 + 2 + 1 = 45$

SOLUTION: **The total number of handshakes is 45.**

Example 2

How many different ways can you make change of 50 cents using only nickels, dimes, and quarters?

STRATEGY: **Use Strategy Number 4: Make a chart or graph.**

STEP 1: Fill in this chart with all the possible ways to make change for 50 cents.

Quarters	Dimes	Nickels
2	0	0
1	2	1
1	1	3
1	0	5
0	5	0
0	4	2
0	3	4
0	2	6
0	1	8
0	0	10

Make this chart in a systematic fashion:
- First, list all the ways to make the change with 2 quarters, then with 1 quarter, and finally no quarters.
- Do the same thing with the dimes and nickels.

STEP 2: Count the number of ways on the chart.

SOLUTION: **There are 10 different ways to make change of 50 cents.**

Example 3

Carole bought a desk that cost $1140. She made a down payment of $300 and will make 7 equal payments to pay for the desk in full. How much will each payment be?

STRATEGY: **Use Strategy Number 2: Make a model. An equation is a kind of model. Write an equation to model the problem.**

STEP 1: Choose a variable for the unknown quantity, the payment.

Let p stand for each payment.

STEP 2: Translate the problem into an equation.

Down payment + 7 × each payment = total cost
$300 + 7 = 1140

STEP 3: Solve the equation.

$300 + 7p = 1140$
$300 - 300 + 7p = 1140 - 300$ (Subtract 300 from each side.)

$0 + 7p = 840$
$7p \times \frac{1}{7} = 840 \times \frac{1}{7}$ (Multiply each side by $\frac{1}{7}$.)
$p = 120$

SOLUTION: **Each payment will be $120.**

Sample Test Questions

1 The mean of 3 numbers is 60, the median of the same 3 numbers is 70, and the mode is 70. What could these 3 numbers be?

A 20, 70, 80

B 30, 70, 80

C 40, 70, 70

D 50, 70, 70

2 How many triangles are in this diagram?

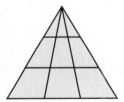

A 17   C 19

B 18   D 20

3 Jack and Joan paint 3 houses every 9 days. At that rate, how many houses can they paint in 30 days?

A 11   C 9

B 10   D 8

4 In how many 3-digit whole numbers between 100 and 1000 does the digit 9 appear in the ones place?

A 19   C 90

B 81   D 100

5 The letters J, K, L stand for digits in the following addition puzzle.

$$\begin{array}{r} JKL \\ + LK \\ \hline JLL \end{array}$$

What does K stand for?

A 0   C 2

B 1   D 3

6 Billy is $\frac{1}{2}$ as old as his sister, $\frac{1}{8}$ as old as his mother, and $\frac{1}{10}$ as old as his father. If the sum of the ages of all four family members is between 75 and 85, how old is Billy?

A 3   C 5

B 4   D 6

7 Nina is twice as old as Daria, and Patty is three times as old as Daria. The sum of Nina's age and Patty's age is 40. How old is Patty?

243

Brief Constructed Response

Lenny is getting 45 cents in change from a purchase.

Part A   How many ways can the cashier make change if there are quarters, dimes, and nickels in the cash register?

Part B   Use what you know about using problem-solving strategies to explain why your answer is correct. Use words and/or numbers to support your explanation.

Lesson

41

Using Reasoning to Solve Problems

In this lesson, you will use logical reasoning to solve such problems as finding a missing digit in a sum or using a pattern to find a missing number or equation.

In one special type of problem, you might be asked to figure out what different sets have in common. For these problems, you will have to know about Venn diagrams.

Venn diagrams consist of circles that stand for sets of elements. These elements can be numbers, letters, people, animals, and many other things.

The circles are usually placed inside a rectangle that is the boundary of all the elements under consideration.

Study this diagram:

7th Graders in Musical Activities

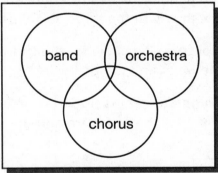

The inside of the rectangle stands for all 7th graders. The three circles show that some 7th graders play in the orchestra, some play in the band, and some sing in the chorus. Notice the overlapping parts. For example, the part of the diagram where the circle for the band overlaps the circle for the chorus means that there are 7th graders who take part in both band and chorus.

You can make conclusions known as generalizations from the information in Venn diagrams.

Example 1

Which of these generalizations can be made from the Venn diagram on the previous page?

A All chorus members are in the band.

B All 7th graders are in either the band or orchestra.

C No chorus member plays in the orchestra and band.

D Some chorus members play in the orchestra and band.

STRATEGY: **Study the diagram as you examine each statement.**

Statement A: Not true. If it were true, then the entire circle for the chorus would be inside the circle for the band.

Statement B: Not true. There are 7th graders in the chorus who are not in the band or orchestra. There are also 7th graders who are not in any of the three activities.

Statement C: Not true. The circle for the chorus overlaps the circles for the band and the orchestra.

Statement D: This statement is true. The circle for the chorus overlaps the circle for the orchestra and the circle for the band.

SOLUTION: **The answer is D.**

The next example is another type of logical reasoning: working a problem backward.

Example 2

If you know that the average of 4 numbers is 13, and the sum of the first 3 numbers is 40, then what is the fourth number?

STRATEGY: **Remember that the average of 4 numbers is the sum of the numbers divided by 4.**

> **STEP 1:** Find the sum of the 4 numbers.
>
> This is the backwards part. We know the average is 13, so we find the sum by multiplying 13 by 4.
> The sum is $13 \times 4 = 52$.
>
> **STEP 2:** Subtract 40 from the sum.
>
> $52 - 40 = 12$

SOLUTION: **The fourth number is 12.**

Here is another example of a problem using logical reasoning.

Example 3

Given these two statements, which conclusion can you make?

> **All pencils come with an eraser.**
> **Donna has a yellow pencil.**

A Donna's pencil does not have an eraser.

B Donna's pencil has an eraser.

C Donna does not have a pencil.

D No conclusion can be made.

STRATEGY: **Read the two statements carefully.**

As you can see, Donna has a pencil. Don't let the "yellow" part of Statement 2 fool you. Donna's pencil must have an eraser, since Statement 1 says all pencils have erasers.

SOLUTION: **The conclusion is B.**

Inductive reasoning is the process of reaching a conclusion based on specific examples.

Example 4

What is the next term in this sequence?

1, 5, 9, 13, ?

STRATEGY: **Use inductive reasoning by looking for a pattern in the specific given terms to reach a conclusion. Each term is 4 greater than the one that comes before it.**

$5 = 1 + \mathbf{4}$
$9 = 5 + \mathbf{4}$
$13 = 9 + \mathbf{4}$

Using inductive reasoning, the next term will be $13 + \mathbf{4}$.

SOLUTION: **The next term in the sequence is 17.**

Deductive reasoning is the process of reaching a conclusion based on known facts.

Example 5

What is the measure of angle a?

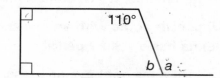

STRATEGY: **Use known facts to reach a conclusion.**

STEP	KNOWN FACT
$90 + 90 + 110 + b = 360$	The sum of the measures of the angles of a quadrilateral is 360.
$290 + b = 360$	$90 + 90 + 110 = 290$
$290 - 290 + b = 360 - 290$	You can subtract the same number from each side of an equation.
$b = 70$	$290 - 290 = 0; 360 - 290 = 70$
$70 + a = 180$	Supplementary angles have a sum of 180.
$70 - 70 + a = 180 - 70$	You can subtract the same number from both sides of an equation.
$a = 110$	$70 - 70 = 0; 180 - 70 = 110$

SOLUTION: $\angle a = 110°$

Sample Test Questions

1 The ◆ in this addition problem must be replaced by what digit?

```
  238
+ 6◆5
─────
  913
```

A 4

B 6

C 7

D 8

2 What additional piece of information do you need to compare the areas of two similar triangles if you know the length of the base and the height of one triangle?

A the height of the second triangle

B the length of a second side of the first triangle

C the perimeter of the second triangle

D none of the above

3 How many different ways can Albert, Barney, Charlie, and David sit in a car if one of them must sit in front and three must sit in back?

A 6

B 12

C 18

D 24

4 What is the twelfth term of the following sequence?

19, 17, 20, 18, 21, 19, 22, 20, 23, ...

A 21

B 22

C 24

D 25

5 Oscar is thinking of 4 numbers. Two of the numbers are 17. The other two numbers differ by 2. The average of the 4 numbers is 18. What are the two missing numbers?

A 10 and 12

B 14 and 16

C 17 and 19

D 18 and 20

6 An equilateral triangle is inscribed in a circle. What do you know about the circle?

A The vertices of the triangle divide the circle into arcs of equal lengths.

B The vertices of the triangle divide the circle into arcs equal in length to the sides of the equilateral triangle.

C The radius of the circle is half the length of any side of the equilateral triangle.

D The diameter of the circle is equal to the length of any side of the equilateral triangle.

7 Given these two statements, which conclusion can you make?

Swimmers like warm weather. Rory is a swimmer.

A Rory does not like warm weather.

B Rory likes warm weather.

C Rory is not a swimmer.

D No conclusion can be made.

8 The Venn diagram below shows the 7th-grade girls who play soccer, basketball, and volleyball. Which of these generalizations can be made from this Venn diagram? (No region is empty.)

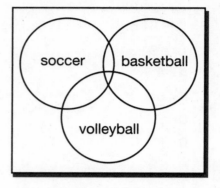

A All basketball players play only one sport.

B All seventh graders play one of the three sports.

C Some volleyball players play soccer and basketball.

D None of the volleyball players plays another sport.

Brief Constructed Response

This figure is a quadrilateral with one side extended.

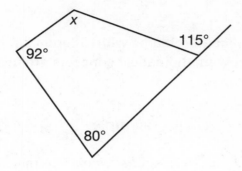

Part A   What is the measure of angle x?

Part B   Use what you know about quadrilaterals, supplementary angles, and deductive reasoning to explain why your answer is correct. Use words and/or numbers to support your explanation.

Lesson 42

Solving Problems

In this lesson you will be solving problems with different kinds of numbers. The following example shows how mathematical concepts are used in finance.

Example

Samantha's mother sells low-risk bonds. Last week, she tallied up how her clients were doing: Monday—lost $30,000; Tuesday—lost $45,000; Wednesday—gained $32,000; Thursday—gained $6,000; and Friday—lost $10,000. Write a sentence showing the gains and losses. How much did her clients gain or lose?

STRATEGY: **Use + and − signs for gains and losses.**

STEP 1: Starting from Monday, find the losses and represent them with negative signs.

Monday: −30,000; Tuesday: −45,000; and Friday: −10,000

STEP 2: Starting from Monday, find the gains and represent them with positive signs.

Wednesday: +32,000; Thursday: +6,000

STEP 3: Write the sum of the gains and losses. Use S as the sum.

$S = (-30,000) + (-45,000) + 32,000 + 6,000 + (-10,000)$

STEP 4: Add the integers.

$(-30,000) + (-45,000) + (-10,000) = -85,000$
$32,000 + 6,000 = 38,000$
$-85,000 + 38,000 = -47,000$

The sum is negative, meaning that there is a net loss for the week.

SOLUTION: **The net loss for the week is $47,000.**

Sample Test Questions

1 On a blueprint, the front wall of a room is $3\frac{3}{4}$ in. and the side wall is $3\frac{3}{8}$ in. How much longer is the front wall in the blueprint?

A $\frac{1}{8}$ in.

B $\frac{1}{4}$ in.

C $\frac{3}{8}$ in.

D $\frac{1}{2}$ in.

2 Which of the following sentences describes this statement: The price of ABC Company started the day at $27, rose $6 the first hour, dropped $4 the second hour, dropped $1.50 the third hour, and dropped $5 the fourth hour.

A $27 + 6 + 4 + 1.50 + 5$

B $27 + 6 + (-4) + 1.50 + (-5)$

C $27 + 6 + (-4) + (-1.50) + (-5)$

D $27 + (-6) + (-4) + (-1.50) + 5$

3 Kristina and her two partners invested in the stock market. After 12 months, their losses came to $75,000. How could they represent the loss for each person?

A $\frac{75,000}{-3}$

B $\frac{-75,000}{3}$

C $\frac{75,000}{3}$

D $\frac{-3}{75,000}$

4 A beaker of salt solution in a chemistry lab is $\frac{2}{5}$ of a liter. A science teacher wants to make 19 times this amount of salt solution. How many liters should she make?

A $19\frac{2}{5}$

B $15\frac{2}{5}$

C $7\frac{4}{5}$

D $7\frac{3}{5}$

5 When Justin was 10 years old, he was 58 inches tall. He is now 15% taller. How many inches tall is he now?

A 62.5

B 64.6

C 66.7

D 67.6

6 About 21% of the total area of Maryland is water. If the total area of Maryland is 12,407 square miles, what is a good estimate of the area of the water?

A 1200

B 2400

C 4800

D 6200

Brief Constructed Response

On Saturday, Georgia completed $\frac{1}{3}$ of her history project. On Sunday, she completed another $\frac{1}{2}$ of what was left to do.

Part A   What fraction was still left after Sunday?

Part B   Use what you know about problem solving to explain why your answer is correct. Use words and/or numbers to support your explanation.

Constructed Response Questions

Brief Constructed Response

1   There were 2540 paying patrons at the first high school basketball game. 35% of them paid $12 per ticket, and the rest of them paid $10 per ticket.

Part A   What was the total income from the tickets?

Part B   Use what you know about problem solving to explain why your answer is correct. Use words and/or numbers to support your explanation.

2   Henry orders food for a snack stand. He took a poll among 100 seventh graders to find their favorite snack. These are the results.

Favorite Snack	Number of People
Peanuts	9
Candy Bars	40
Potato Chips	30
Pretzels	9
Ice Cream	12

Part A   Based on the results in the table above, if Henry orders 300 bags of potato chips, how many candy bars should he order?

Part B   Use what you know about data and making predictions to explain why your answer is correct. Use words and/or numbers to support your explanation.

255

Extended Constructed Response

3   A TV set had a regular price of $740. It was put on sale at a 30% discount. When the TV set didn't sell, its price was reduced to 30% off the already discounted price.

Part A   What was the total dollar amount of the discount?

Part B
- Use what you know about finding the percent of a total to explain why your answer is correct. Use words and/or numbers to support your explanation.
- Suppose the regular price had just one reduction of 60%. How would the discount compare with the discount after two 30% discounts? Use words and/or numbers to explain your answer.